AF255709

Building Your Digital Sanctuary

Building Your Digital Sanctuary

An Introductory Guide to Effective Digital Ministry

Edited by Brandan J. Robertson

CASCADE *Books* · Eugene, Oregon

BUILDING YOUR DIGITAL SANCTUARY
An Introductory Guide to Effective Digital Ministry

Copyright © 2023 Wipf and Stock Publishers. All rights reserved. Except for brief quotations in critical publications or reviews, no part of this book may be reproduced in any manner without prior written permission from the publisher. Write: Permissions, Wipf and Stock Publishers, 199 W. 8th Ave., Suite 3, Eugene, OR 97401.

Cascade Books
An Imprint of Wipf and Stock Publishers
199 W. 8th Ave., Suite 3
Eugene, OR 97401

www.wipfandstock.com

PAPERBACK ISBN: 978-1-6667-1899-7
HARDCOVER ISBN: 978-1-6667-1900-0
EBOOK ISBN: 978-1-6667-1901-7

Cataloguing-in-Publication data:

Names: Robertson, Brandan J., editor.

Title: Building your digital sanctuary : an introductory guide to effective digital ministry / edited by Brandan J. Robertson.

Description: Eugene, OR: Cascade Books, 2023 | Includes bibliographical references.

Identifiers: ISBN 978-1-6667-1899-7 (paperback) | ISBN 978-1-6667-1900-0 (hardcover) | ISBN 978-1-6667-1901-7 (ebook)

Subjects: LCSH: Digital media—Religious aspects—Christianity | Social media—Religious aspects—Christianity

Classification: BV652.95 .R50 2023 (print) | BV652.95 .R50 (ebook)

02/06/23

Contents

Introduction

Rev. Brandan Robertson

The world has changed more in the past thirty years than it has changed in the past six thousand years. It is rare that we take time to think about just how fundamentally different the world has been transformed since the dawn of the internet for public use in 1993. A majority of the world is now connected in ways that have never been possible in human history—in real time, we can speak with, share information with, and collaborate with virtually anyone, anywhere in the world. This instantaneous connection has supercharged the rate of technological innovation which has led to the creation of widespread access to technology that once was only possible in science fiction.

Personally, I've never known a world other than this one. I was born in 1992, and by the time I was a six, we had a computer in our house and in my schools equipped with dial-up internet that allowed for *some degree* of connection to the world. I can't even imagine what it was like to live in a pre-internet, pre-computer world. I can hardly remember what it was like not to have a smart phone. Yet this interconnected, virtual world that we all are now living in is still *brand new* and the implications of this technological revolution and perhaps *evolution* of humanity have yet to be fully realized.

From the earliest days of the internet, religious leaders and communities have pondered about what this could mean for their own theology, spiritual practice, and way of being religious in the world. Since as early as 2002, the Vatican has been commenting on the emergence of a spiritual cyberspace as inevitable but inadequate to fully enrich the spiritual lives of the world's Catholics.[1] Similarly, in 2004, sociologists Lorne Dawson and Douglas Cowan published "Religion Online: Finding Faith on the Internet" which urged religious communities to explore and adapt to the internet and other emerging technologies, lest they risk losing touch with their congregations in the emerging virtual world. Yet despite this early engagement at the intersection of religion and the internet, religious communities have unsurprisingly been slow to adopt and adapt to the opportunities presented to them by the internet.

The late Phyllis Tickle wrote that every five hundred years, humanity undergoes a great reformation—or "rummage sale", as Tickle put it—that fundamentally alters how humanity moves forward. According to Tickle's measurement, the last great reformation began roughly in 1517 when Martin Luther launched the Protestant Reformation and the printing press made mass communication possible for the first time in history, and just over five hundred years later, humanity has, undoubtably, undergone it's greatest evolution yet, thanks to the COVID-19 global pandemic of 2020, which forced nearly every sector of human life around the world online in a matter of weeks. If faith communities were to survive in the midst of the pandemic, they had no choice but to figure out how to create community and worship experiences online. In a matter of weeks, a majority of the world transitioned to live into a fully virtual reality. For as much terror and loss as the COVID-19 pandemic wrought around the world, I think it is safe to say that the impact of the pandemic on the interconnectedness of humanity was a net positive.

Which brings us to the point of this book—I was pastoring a church in San Diego, California when the pandemic began, and though I have grown up with the internet and am very proficient in digital technology, the Sunday that we canceled our in-person

1. Catholic Church. Pontificium Consilium de Communicationibus Socialibus. (2002). *Ethics in communications.* Città del Vaticano: Libreria editrice vaticana. ISBN 8820972786. OCLC 50798819.

services and attempted to conduct our first virtual service was a terrifying trainwreck. Our church had not invested in livestreaming or web conferencing technology, and so the only equipment we had to stream anything was our cell phones which could stream to Facebook Live.

That first livestreamed Sunday, when our congregation and indeed the entire country was terrified about what we were about to endure with the pandemic and was longing for community and connection, our livestream failed numerous times due to poor Wi-Fi in our church sanctuary, the audio was terrible, and only a fourth of our community actually figured out how to access the service on our Facebook page.

Over the next six months, we slowly improved the quality of our livestream and worked to ensure our community knew how to connect to our service each week, but as the leader of this community I grew increasingly dismayed that I had not prepared our community to go virtual long before this pandemic began. A relatively small investment of a few thousand dollars would have prepared us to have been engaging compellingly online like many other of the more conservative religious communities had been doing, not as preparation for a pandemic but as a way to reach more people where they were. And now, in this dire moment where we were faced with the choice of either going digital or potentially ceasing to exist as a church community, I had no guide to help me think through *how* to effectively become a virtual community.

This book is meant to be that guide—a short, practical introduction for religious communities to begin thinking through how they can develop a robust "digital sanctuary," a space for folks to connect, worship, and grow on the internet. While most communities figured out how to become virtual to some degree over the course of the pandemic, many have still not invested serious time, resources, or attention to building out their digital ministry as a vital pillar of the work of their communities. If communities abandon the digital ministries they developed during the pandemic and revert to being primarily "in-person" communities, I believe they are quite literally hastening their own demise and failing to be faithful stewards of what they have to offer the spiritual seekers of the world. It is imperative that we work together to discover ways to exist as hybrid communities if we are going to continue to remain healthy, flourishing communities in the decades to come.

This emerging new era requires us to rethink and reform how we imagine the mission of our faith communities and how they will express our ancient faith for an ever-evolving world. It is my prayer that the wisdom and experience presented in this book by a wide array of ministry professionals will be a starting point and a launching pad for faith leaders and people of faith alike as they seek to discover how they might herald the good news and cultivate meaningful community in this dawning digital era of human history. There is no one-size-fits-all approach to digital ministry, but there are tried-and-true techniques and practices that can help faith communities begin to build meaningful and impactful digital sanctuaries in their contexts.

May you and your community be challenged, equipped, and inspired by the words of this guide as you cross the threshold of what promises to be the most revolutionary period of human history.

Soli Deo Gloria.

I

Rethinking Worship

Rev. Bailey Brawner

I'll be honest with you. I'm going through a bit of an identity crisis as I'm writing this. I spent the first twenty-eight years of my life in the local church, leading in paid and unpaid capacities since I was old enough to read Scripture from the pulpit. I went to seminary at Boston University, then went on to pastor in both Alaska and California. At the end of 2021, I stepped away from what I had always known church to be. And while church isn't about the building, that was how I knew to worship best. Now, here I am, working a 9–5, having traditional weekends and a semblance of work/life boundaries.

With these "perks" also comes the aforementioned identity crisis. For so long, I identified strongly with the job that I did. Pastor or Reverend would replace my name, and I felt this innate connection to the work itself, which upon reflection, probably had more to do with the lack of boundaries often at play in faith communities and less to do with how closely I felt I was following my call to ministry. For so long, the job I did kept me close to God too. This isn't to say that I don't know how to experience God outside the local church, but my faith and worship has dramatically shifted now that I no longer identify as a 'professional Christian', to use my friend Sarah Heath's language.

Why then am I, a used-to-be pastor, writing this chapter on rethinking worship? Why am I, skeptical, cynical, fully convinced of the institutional brokenness in the church, the person who is sharing my insight on rethinking worship? I don't pretend to be the only person who can speak on this, but also I have spent enough of my life surrounded by worship that I can tell what it is, and maybe more importantly, what it isn't. We're going to explore that more together in this section, and as we do, I invite you to consider the way your identity connects with the understanding of worship you've always known, and perhaps the ways you feel called to explore a deeper understanding of worship.

At its core, worship deals innately with identity, that is, more specifically, how we can and do identify with the Divine. Each of us worship in different ways and for different reasons, but in doing so, there's this element of connecting with something bigger than ourselves. We do that connecting work in many different ways; fellowship, relationship building, music, liturgy, Scripture, preaching, and the list goes on. We want to find new ways or familiar ways to identify with that thing which is bigger than us. And that is what worship is about at its bare bones. It's about feeling a sense of pull or call to try to understand your place in this world a little bit better.

When the COVID-19 pandemic started, there was so much we did not know. I was in my first year serving as senior pastor of a church in San Diego, California. I had a staff of ten, a congregation who was just beginning to trust me as their pastor, and our congregation was going through an important visioning process about who they wanted to be as a worshiping community.

"Here is the church. Here is the steeple. Open the doors, and see all the people."

If you're like me, this simple rhyme has helped to inform your faith community of what worship should be like. And if you're really like me, you've got some pretty cool hand gestures to match.

Since the first instances of church, there's been a huge emphasis on the physical space, the steeple, the walls, the altar—those are things that have been assumed to make worship what it is. When you were to ask someone what church they went to, they'd give you the name of a place with a physical location, "Kenai UMC on Frontage Road," or "First Church by the post office", they'd tell you.

What happens, then, when the physical space goes away? Two possibilities. First, the change can cause the community to crumble. This can happen for many reasons, including financial hardship, shifts in leadership abilities, new demographics, etc. And the second possibility, the one my congregation discovered, is that removing the physical space allowed us to thrive, to live into the community God created us to be.

As I'm rereading that last sentence, it sounds a little bit like a fairy tale. They all lived happily ever after? Not quite. We had our fair share of frustrations, shortcomings, learning curves, and failed attempts. But the way we were able to get through it was remembering that our identity has always been and will always be bigger than a building. So together, myself, my staff, and our congregants worked to make worship bigger and more all-encompassing than an hour-long service once a week. And I'll be honest, the ways we did that, the changes we made, they really pissed some people off. But it was more important to create opportunities for all people to experience the Divine than to keep a few people comfortable.

So if you're reading this, you may be looking to step further into the space of digital sanctuary too. You may be completely unfamiliar with the possibilities available to translate this form of worship you've always done into a new thing. In reflection and prayer, the thing I keep coming back to is identity. When we remember who we are and whose we are, we will learn that our scope of worship is much larger and goes much deeper than the physical sanctuary has ever given us credit for.

In the next few pages, I want to lay out some practical things you can easily implement into your existing worship structures to allow more digital engagement, whether you're a hybrid community who is navigating both the physical and digital spaces, a fully online church, or are just interested in getting your (digital) feet wet. Feel free to pick and choose what works for your people and context and adapt these tools to further shape your community's identity. I named these three sections based on what I've learned to be some of the most valuable purposes for worship, both for me and others I've spoken to. The sections are Worship as Engagement, Worship as Leadership, and Worship as Getting Out of God's Way.

Worship as Engagement

Do you remember the old adage that asks the question about the tree falling in a forest but nobody is there to hear it? It reminds me an awful lot of the conversations I was having as we discussed how to begin this transition online for worship. We had decided to worship via Facebook Live, and had learned (mostly by multiple failures) how to livestream and piece together our regular worship service parts. We decided to combine live elements such as the preaching, prayer time, and offering with pre-recorded elements like our time for Young Leaders, music, and Scripture reading. We started very low-tech, so folks quickly got used to my grainy face coming from my laptop in my living room. It was bare bones, but it fit our vision and our theology. Those often are the hardest places to start when doing a new thing. How can we translate what we did to fit this new challenge that has been thrust upon us? So we solved the practical, but the major problem we quickly discovered is that the engagement was no longer something we could measure or even encourage.

This was a problem that was revealed to us because we knew the purpose and vision of worship for our community. Ultimately, what was important for our congregation and for me as the one tasked with leading that vision, was that we felt both connected to God and to each other. Those rituals of Scripture, music, preaching, and prayer were serving the purpose of connecting us to God, but when we couldn't see one another in the sanctuary like we used to, there was a disconnect and even some mourning of 'what church used to be like'.

In the visioning sessions just weeks prior to our physical sanctuary shutting down, the congregation adopted the following mission statement: "Loving God by Loving All: Connecting Faith and Community through Worship and Serving Others". These fourteen words told me exactly what our next step needed to be as a community transitioning online. It revealed to me that what my community cared about in regard to worship was worship as engagement and connection. It meant that for me as the senior pastor to lead my congregation into this next chapter, they needed to have a sense of connection to hold on to, a sense of togetherness. Up until this point, that connecting point had been the building, so I had to be creative.

One of the first things I did was utilize the comments section during our livestreams. You may be thinking, duh, but let me be clear that I never promised ingenuity, just practicality. Every Sunday at 10 AM, I'd welcome folks in the comments section, saying hello and what the Scripture was, pasting in our mission statement, making a corny joke, talking about the weather, etc. I wanted to get a conversation started. Each week, more and more people would say hello, and some of the lay leadership would consistently welcome individuals whose first time it was, or ask a question to the group to get the banter flowing. This commenting ritual became so important for us, because it told a story of who we were, not just a group of people who needed everything to be perfect or the same every week. We were a group of humans from so many different backgrounds, who chose to come together in worship to connect.

Throughout our livestreamed service, I'd always be looking for ways to invite participation and engagement. And our staff began to find their own ways to do this as well. When I was sharing the children's message, I'd say something like "if you are a young leader, this is a special message for you, so feel free to come closer to the screen to hear it". It replaced the time in the service when the young people would come and sit on the steps of the altar area, and it let them know that they were valuable to us.

We'd invite folks to share joys and concerns in the comments section and would also give them the chance to DM us if they had a more confidential request. This prayer time was important to the community, as prayer was one of the means of connection they felt to each other and to God during the worship service. We would read aloud the prayer requests then say aloud the Lord's Prayer with the rest of the community from our homes.

As my congregation would tell you, not everything was received well the first time I implemented it. If you're a part of congregations like mine, participation in worship sometimes feels like pulling teeth. When we worshiped in person, I asked folks to share something aloud once or twice during the sermon portion, and it absolutely pained people to do so. But as someone who studied to be an elementary school teacher, I have the gift of patience, so I'd wait it out and gently encourage a response or two. Each week, when I'd write my sermons for our livestream worship services, I'd ask myself, how do I want folks to interact with this message or this text? I wanted them to be an active participant, feeling as close to the old normal as possible, even though many had swapped their Sunday best for their pajamas on the couch.

Throughout my ten- to fifteen-minute sermon, I'd ask about three questions throughout. The first was usually more of an icebreaker question. Let's pretend this is a message about our identity in Christ. My first question might be "what word would your best friend use to describe you?" I'd talk a little more, digging into the Scripture lesson, then pause for the next question, where I aimed to form connection points between the hearer of the message and something related to the Scripture. And then the third question would always give them a moment to reflect on what they could take with them, from the worship service and into the world. In this same imaginary sermon, I might ask them how they could use the gifts and identity God has given them to be a disciple in the world. After each question, I would pause and wait for folks to comment. There was always about a fifteen-second delay from when I'd say something and when the livestream would hear it, so I'd ask the question a second time, or answer it myself until I could read some of the comments out loud. It made me feel like I was having a conversation with the congregation, and it helped them to feel present, like they were committing to worship, not just having it on as background noise while doing the dishes.

A huge moment of discovery for me began after we started gaining some traction through social media. I had started developing a following on TikTok, and folks there would start to join the church for worship on Sundays. Our San Diego congregation quickly became global, with some of our most active participants being from other countries, like Nicole in Australia and Erika in France. While chatting with one of our members, they casually mentioned how funny it was that I would begin the service by saying good morning. I laughed, because it had never occurred to me that there were some people who were worshiping in places where it wasn't the morning. Even our East Coasters had already had lunch by the time we began the service. I learned how to adapt my language to be more inclusive of the community we had developed and nurtured together. In the same way that progressive churches will shift their "boys and girls" language to "y'all" as a way of addressing people, going digital means that the audience you will reach will be looking to be seen. Connecting with the people in your care isn't just a pastoral care 101 tool. It's a means of welcome and evangelism.

How might you engage the community you lead in a new way that requires them to be seen even more?

Worship as Leadership

I'm a millennial, which means that on TikTok, I'm seen as old. But in the church world, I'm practically a baby. This means that I started on third base when many of my clergy colleagues had started on first base. I was more prepared to handle a fully digital worship space when that reality was thrust upon us. I was one of the few who were knowledgeable about different streaming platforms, how to connect new cameras via Bluetooth, and could edit together parts of a worship service to seem semi-cohesive. As a queer person, I also know the internet to be a place for building and finding community. My first coming out experiences happened in my Twitter feed far before I could come out to people face-to-face. And so for me, creating the space was never the most challenging aspect of rethinking worship. The most challenging part was leading others to see the value of worship fully online.

A great grandmother, a second grader, and a trans man walked into a Zoom room. It's not the beginning of a terrible joke. It was, however, the reality of our worship community. From the start, our congregation was a group of older folks, mostly white, straight, upper-middle class. Our church building neighbored an elementary school, so we had several families who'd attend worship. And as we started expanding our reach online, more younger folks began joining us too, mostly LGBTQIA+ folks. Like many of you, we went through the pandemic cycles when it came to digital worship. First, when our two-week quarantine started, people craved community but were still discovering how to do that well. My checking-in phone calls with our older members turned into phone tutorials on how to create a Facebook account and where to search our church's name to find the worship service. Our staff meetings had a lot to do with the ways things would be edited together or how they'd appear on a digital stage. That next stage following was where Zoom fatigue hit. This affected our kids most significantly, who were spending six hours a day on their laptops listening to a teacher who was just as over it as the teachers themselves were. Family members were overwhelmed and stretched too thin trying to add the role of educator and IT into their child's life. Many other pandemic cycles came after, each bringing its own unique challenges and opportunities for growth in regards to worship.

Being a leader through these many cycles was so hard because we were dealing with so many unique situations and people groups. You know as well as I do that it's impossible to make everyone happy, especially in the church, but it took on a whole other level now, because we weren't just dealing with people's preferences. We were also dealing with differing levels of ability to worship in a particular fashion. We played around with using other social media platforms to stream from. The determining factor for using Facebook Live had nothing to do with it being the best. It simply was the most user friendly way to host a worshipful space. Our goal was to get everyone on the same page, or at the very least, reading the same genre of book. Because of the staff of ten I had, that started internally, with our leadership.

The biggest thing we as leaders needed to tailor was our language surrounding worship. Of course, we had initially thought this was just going to be a two week thing, that we'd be back in the building by Easter. We would say things like "going back to normal" or "online worship" as qualifiers, as if to say "not the real kind of worship." Soon we realized that things weren't going back to normal, not as we knew it to be anyways. We had to adapt quickly and find ways to communicate that who we were now, worshiping through screens, was not any less valid and was not any less holy than how we had been worshiping two weeks, two months, or even two years ago.

That shift as leaders not only helped us to embrace the challenge of digital worship. It also helped us to be a more inclusive worship community as a whole. We had a sort of fresh start, like walking into a new home and deciding how you'll decorate it. We could do anything we wanted, because we had a blank canvas in front of us. And because nothing had ever been done even remotely similarly to what we were moving into, those preconceived notions of what worship is or is not did not come with the territory. Our staff joked early on that the bar was low, because literally anything would be better than nothing at all, which is what many of our folks assumed when they heard the church was closing due to COVID. We learned that the demographic of people we were worshiping with was no longer mostly straight, white people in a ten-mile radius. And so, we needed to stop treating our worship like that was the case. We stopped singling out new people, encouraged our congregation to ask more inclusive questions and avoid assuming who someone is and what they've experienced based on what their perceived gender, age, or occupation is. We created systems of radical welcome that connected people who would have had no business interacting together in any other world. And that intentional work from our leaders, both the staff and the ones who rose to the occasion as worshippers—it created a worship home for so many.

One of my favorite means of worship, and unlikely relationships formed within it, was at an expression of worship we started called Dinner Church. Every other Tuesday evening, we opened a Zoom room with no agenda other than sacred community. We had a few of our regulars, mostly older folks, who would join consistently. One week, a younger, newer member named Addison worshipped with us at Dinner Church, where they met Bill, one of the older regulars. Bill and Addison laughed together about tennis, Taylor Swift, and internet jargon. In the hour they spent together, they worshipped hard together, and it was beautiful to witness. The next time we met together, I texted our younger people group chat and invited people to join if they wanted. Addison replied immediately, asking if Bill would be there, because if he would, then everyone has to go because he's the best, they said. This unlikely pairing, and the sharing surrounding their experiences together in worship, helped others to find a home there too. They felt connection and home, sourced from the Divine, and together they found common ground because God had never left.

I share this in the leadership section, not because I had anything remotely significant to do with Bill and Addison's friendship, but because I want to encourage you to continue practicing that ministry of presence when you are leading worship. You don't need fancy cameras, agendas, or music to worship in a holy way. You simply need to be willing to show up and pay attention to where God is speaking into the lives of those in your care.

Being a leader in these times, rethinking worship, is all about being a learner. When you know intimately the needs of your people, the goals of your context, and the gifts each person brings, it will become clear to you what the next steps are. And if it's not clear to you, then perhaps it will be to the other leaders around you, even and especially the ones whose gifts haven't yet been recognized. You as a leader in this place are uniquely qualified and called. You know your people and their needs better than anyone else, and they trust you to be consistent in the vision and identity that their worship space needs and desires. Give yourself the grace you need and the support you need to get started.

May you trust yourself as a leader, not because you are perfect, but because you care about your people. May you find ways to make your worship space home again for some and a new home entirely for others. And may you examine the biases and assumptions we have carried for too long that we have now received permission to let go of, making more room at the digital table for all to feel important, needed, and radically welcomed.

Worship as Getting Out of God's Way

I saved this one for last because it's the one I find most annoying. And unironically, it's the one I find to be the truest for my own life. I realized my call to ministry precisely at the same time as I got out of God's way. I remember being in college studying elementary education. I knew I was called to lead in some ministry capacity, and I had a hunch it was to pastor, but frankly, I was scared and stubborn. So I did the logical thing, try and make a deal with God. I decided I'd compromise because that's how every good call story goes, right? In a conversation with God, I said "Yeah sure, I'll be in ministry. But like, as a kids Sunday school teacher. That way, I finish my degree and don't waste that time. You wouldn't want that for my life, right God?" . . . yikes.

The following summer, I got hired on to be an intern at my home church. I had assumed I'd be leading Vacation Bible School, doing some office work, and planning lessons for Sunday school. So imagine my surprise, when one of the pastors came into my office one afternoon, asking me if I'd preach the following Sunday. My mind said absolutely not. I tried so hard to get out of it. I remember screaming in my car for the fifteen-minute drive home from work in hopes that I'd lose my voice in time for Sunday. Sadly, not even a full-on Jesse McCartney concert in my SUV could get me out of it, so I showed up, ready to preach. I walked up to the pulpit, body shaking, sweating profusely. I started to speak. And if you thought my body was shaking, it was nothing compared to my voice. I couldn't tell you the words that came out of my mouth, but once they came out, it clicked. I remember thinking "oh shit, this is what I'm supposed to do". Glamorous, right?

I kicked and screamed even more the following years, and continue doing so, even well into my twenties. Still, I received clarity and was able to see what God was calling me to do and be when I got out of God's way. Giving up control is among the purest forms of worship because it allows God to be God.

Theologically speaking, our job is not to bring God to anyone or manipulate a space or community to see God in a specific manner. I don't care how highly you regard your ability to share a good message. We get into a really sticky territory if we think that we as faith leaders can 'bring' God to a space, whether that be a building, a Zoom room, or a foreign country (if you know, you know). If that were our job, we'd be called gatekeepers, not disciples. We are in the business of creating opportunities for others (and ourselves) to recognize God in their midst. Sometimes, we do this, and other times, our intention and design for worship is nothing like we had planned. But as a recovering perfectionist and someone who tries to control everything, I know from experience that we simply cannot choose or plan or control the way God will show up in our lives. (You can reread my call story above if you need to.) And truly thank God for that, right? Because our own perception of who God (or whatever name you give the Divine) is is limited and it is far too small to be who God is for everyone.

So here's the biggest thing I can offer to you when it comes to rethinking worship in digital spaces: Remember that mistakes, just as much and often more so than your most intricately planned liturgy, are opportunities for the people in your care to encounter the Divine. Let go of control, the expectations of yourself and others, the overplanning, the timelines with no flexibility, and allow God to be God. Think about those worshipful moments I'm sure you've had where the baby cries when you're preaching that sounds like a resounding AMEN. Or recall the times when even your most perfect recitation of a Scripture verse was far less helpful to a grieving family than simply being present in their home. Oftentimes, the most sacred and holy ways we can lead is by allowing ourselves to step back, and letting God do the rest. Let your Wi-Fi issues be an opportunity for silence, your autocorrect fails be moments for laughter, and your learnings be their own form of liturgy and healing.

Friends, you are invited to show up as your full self, carrying your truest of identities. You are invited to try new things, to fail with grace as often as you can, to have a sense of humor, to know your limits, to rely on the wisdom of others, and ultimately, to rethink what you know and instead ask what could be. You are invited to look beyond the confines of tradition, of what we've always done, and instead, hold true to the identity of the beloved community in which you serve.

Let's worship together.

Bailey Brawner (she/her) is a queer author and content creator, who does work at the intersectionality of sexuality and spirituality. She lives with her partner, Dani, and their fur children: Taylor, Oakley, Riley, and Charli. Bailey is a self-identified "ex-pastor", who worked in churches up until the end of 2021. She now 'pastors' on social media, creating spiritual spaces for those hurt by the church, namely her LGBTQIA+ siblings. You can connect with Bailey and her work on social media at @baileynbrawner.

2

Fostering Digital Community

Rev. Matthew Hambrick

It started with a phone call.

"Bro."

My friend always calls me bro. He is a pastor serving in a neighboring community and is always good for a hot take. This time he was about to come out with the hottest take I'd ever heard.

"None of this online stuff is real."

The online "stuff" he was talking about was online worship, online community groups, and even video chat prayer gatherings. At the time he said this, both of us had been leading our church communities online for nearly three months because of the pandemic lockdown. It was true—due to not being able to minister with congregation members in person, the ministry had begun to feel less real, less honest, and less connected than it ever had. I remember trying to remind myself "there is nothing new under the sun" (Eccl 1:9). There have often been times in history when people have been kept apart by circumstances. In the Bible, the apostle Paul lamented not being able to see the Roman church in person (Rom 1:11). Then about the Thessalonian church and their continued separation, he wrote that it was so bad that it felt like they'd been "orphaned" (1 Thess 2:17). Paul was incredibly effective at building his churches from afar and even he struggled to feel good about being distant from his people. My friend and I had done our best, but the tension that came from trying to lead our congregations into the digital realm was rising, and the cracks were starting to show.

Why Does a Pastor Need to Build Digital Community?

This season had proved so difficult that I had started wondering why I should continue to work so hard to make digital community happen in my small mainline congregation. My pews had been full of people from neighboring cities who commuted into the neighborhood. Apart from the church sanctuary, they were not connected by a collective sense of place. Since they couldn't worship in that sanctuary in person, why shouldn't they just move their mouse over to one of the thousands of church websites from congregations much larger and better resourced than mine? Wouldn't they get better music, better sermons, and more small-group opportunities than our church could ever offer? If digital community was just about increasing access to online worship during the pandemic lockdown, then there were already plenty of other opportunities available at large churches that had already started that outreach years before there was a need. Why not just send a link each week to the best preaching I could find and connect anyone who asked for a small group to a larger church I trusted? After pondering that possibility, I concluded that small congregations like mine may need digital community even more than people in larger churches. That realization called into question every decision I had made around technology in the church. If I knew that my people commuted from an average of thirty minutes away, why had I not worked harder to integrate remote attendance before now?

Large churches often offer a one-size-fits-all approach that can leave out the kind of person who make their way to a smaller congregation like mine. Over the years, my people had stayed a part of their church through all the seasons of ups and downs because it offered them a sense of closeness and community that was uniquely tailored to them. It felt safe. They often called their church a family. Knowing that my parishioners lived all around the county made me realize that when a smaller church offers online ministries, it can obviously provide an opportunity to foster meaningful relationships for people who live geographically close to the brick-and-mortar location, but it can also provide opportunities to connect people who might attend because they appreciate what the church is already offering and the people who made it happen. This second group may never attend the church or its programs in person. They may even live many thousands of miles away.

The same apostle Paul who hated to be separated from his people would have likely loved Zoom. He used the best technology available to him at the time, letter writing, to reach people and build communities across his world. I can't help but imagine that he would have constantly had Zoom sessions going with all his people spread across the continent. I believe he would have embraced the medium as a third space that would enable him to reach people not interested in the traditional means and models by which community had been built by the church in the past. By embracing these new modes of communication, we can also encounter people left out by all the barriers to church attendance. The one who will never show up on Sunday morning may be willing to show up on Zoom in their pajamas on Monday morning.

When people visit a church for the first time, there are so many unknowns. They might wonder if someone will greet them at the door with kindness or find a place to sit. Then when considering the sermon and church teachings, they might fear that the teaching may be strange or judgmental. Going deeper, many of our church gathering traditions are built for extroverts, e.g., introducing visitors, shaking hands during the service, and the pressure to mingle at coffee hour after worship. Joining a digital space takes away some of the barriers and may lessen anxiety. If the experience becomes too intense, it's not necessary to awkwardly walk out to get away. One simply needs to press "Leave" on the Zoom app.

Because the first horribly produced worship services and several empty Zoom rooms were still fresh in my memory, it would have been easy to just agree with my pastor friend and admit that none of this online "stuff" was "real." It would have been convenient for me to believe him so that I would not have to look in the mirror and feel like a failure. By conceding that all our interactions online were less than real, I could pretend that I no longer needed to worry about it. I could just sit back, relax, and wait for the world to reopen, and for God to show up again. But I couldn't admit my friend was right because I had already felt the realness of an online community long before the pandemic.

How Is a Digital Community Built?

1. To Grow Closer the Group Must Be Small

I began seminary in 2014 at an institution that had recently begun using a hybrid model of instruction. Students would gather in person for a week or two and then return to their homes to work remotely for the rest of the semester. Like many other seminaries, the time of in-person instruction was an amazing opportunity to meet other students and to interact directly with the professor. Time in the classroom provided space for conversation and conflict. It allowed students to talk over one another and argue theological points and ministry methodologies. Students were able to make friends and, often, enemies as well, but then they went home to finish the semester.

Surprisingly, once students arrived at home, that was often when the magic began. Some instructors had an incredible talent for online community building. They were excellent at curating online spaces that provided a road map for students to go deeper with one another. The best classes were the ones in which the professors knew that to successfully facilitate the connection between students, the groups had to be smaller. They had to give up everything they thought they knew about what constituted a classroom. Of course, there were classes in which the professor had neither the skill nor the interest to make community happen in their online classes. These classes did not feel real, in any sense of the word, and my friend's criticism would have held true in those cases. While some professors would just record a video lecture with them standing in front of a white board for forty-five minutes, other professors knew their methods had to change. In an online world where Netflix is just a moment of boredom and a browser click away, it is essential to make the material as engaging and interactive as possible.

2. Digital Community Can Feel Real

Digital community is as real as we let it become. My first class at seminary required that every person belong to a small group to share and facilitate spiritual practices. It was just thirty minutes each week on video chat, but the results were often remarkable. My group would meet early on Monday morning, before the day had a chance to break into our lives. Then a member of the group would offer a meditation or a prayer in a style that was unfamiliar to the rest of the group. I would leave that digital space each week feeling awakened to spiritual possibility. Those connections first formed on Zoom led to real, long-term friendships that continue today. This digital small group was real because we treated it like it was real. Because we were guided by a professor who understood the power of this medium, we were encouraged to treat it seriously. This method became my model when I began gathering small groups in person, and it became especially important later when I had to move these small groups onto digital platforms.

When my church faced the reality of the pandemic, it wasn't hard to realize that if we tried to transition our in-person worship and small-group experiences directly into an online presence, it would not translate. I worried about what would happen if I put a camera at the back of the room and led worship just like it had been done before the pandemic, acting like nothing had changed. The best-case scenario was for that would be we would suffer through it until we could come back to in-person gatherings. The worst-case scenario would be that no one would attend because they would agree that it didn't feel real, that it felt like a puppet show version of what they had known. We needed to make significant adjustments to ensure we were reaching people where they were, which was often in their living rooms or bedrooms. I realized that I might even need to consider starting all these programs from scratch, built completely for the internet age and the pandemic era.

Fortunately, I had already started a small group back in 2018 that would help the church move forward while we were unable to gather in person. It began ten months after I became the pastor in San Diego because one of the longtime members of the congregation, Eleanor, approached me and asked if it would be possible to start a theologically minded reading group. Of course, I loved her idea. There is something special about reading a book one chapter at a time with a group of people who are taking it as seriously as you are. To plan out the details, Eleanor and I grabbed coffee and talked over what we wanted to read and who we would like to target as an audience. We decided that our goal would be to include people from our congregation who were not otherwise involved in another ministry. We would hold the group in a local coffee shop so that we could begin to know our neighbors better.

What emerged was a book group devoted to reading controversial Christian women authors. The first book we read was *Accidental Saints* by Nadia Bolz-Weber. We would eventually name the group "Accidental Saints" in honor of that first work. So began several years of reading collaboratively. We read Nadia Bolz-Weber, Rachel Held Evans, Diana Butler Bass, and many others in a coffee shop just down the street from the church. It was an amazing time of being together and thinking in public. That said, being a multigenerational church in an affluent neighborhood, the people in our small group would often be away on vacation or simply traveling to see friends or grown children. Because of my seminary experience, group video chat always resided in the background of my mind as an option to solve scheduling problems. For those times when a few people would need to be gone, it would be no bother to jump on group video chat for a week or two as a stop-gap measure.

Accordingly, when March 2020 came along, our group easily pivoted completely to online video chat and continued on, almost like nothing had changed. Each Monday morning instead of the coffee shop down the street, we gathered in a Zoom room that never changed its meeting ID and, despite the risk of internet trolls potentially finding our room, the group left its digital doors unlocked so that anyone could join the conversation.

That Zoom room became the front doors of our church. It became the church office hours. It even acted as the church social hall. It was all these things rolled into one. Once the pandemic began, many more people were available on Monday mornings, and the group grew significantly. It grew because so many people were working from home and were often looking for an opportunity to rebuild a sense of community that had been lost due to the lockdown. With the rise of the pandemic and its resulting exile, the online group called Accidental Saints became the centerpiece of my church's outreach. Though the core group remained the same, new members joined almost weekly from across the United States and took the opportunity to bond together over books they may have never heard of, and authors whose voices may have never made it to their own faith communities.

It was during this time that Madeline found us. Madeline, a forty-something professional coach, who lived nearly an hour's drive away, came to her first online gathering of Accidental Saints just two months into the pandemic. When the lockdown started, she realized that she had a unique opportunity. She had wanted to leave mainstream evangelicalism behind, wanted to leave the church she had attended for the past five years. Under normal circumstances leaving your church can be quite difficult. A close-knit community always notices your absence. Madeline realized that by being unable to attend in person, she was enabled to shop around without hurting her current congregation. Further, she said she realized that there was never a better opportunity to look for a new church because, for the first time ever, almost every congregation had their worship service online. Those first few weeks, because of the boredom of lockdown and her desperation to find a community she could call home, she and her husband would attend multiple worship services each Sunday morning.

Madeline had recently begun the process of deconstructing her faith. By that, she meant that she was dissecting her faith so she could look more closely at each part, asking herself whether the belief was true or helpful, or whether it might even be harmful. She was stripping away all the pieces that no longer proved true. Though this happens in various Christian traditions, in Madeline's church, this process was viewed as harmful, and any person who engaged in deconstruction was considered to be lacking in faith. In churches like hers, deconstruction is discouraged because it often accompanies criticism of church leaders. Knowing this, she was looking for a congregation that would be open to someone like her, someone who would likely have a lot of questions and potentially some well-deserved criticism.

After hours of Google searching, she came across my church's website and, since we made it was clear that we were a progressive church, she decided to discretely attend online worship. During normal times, this would have been a big step, but with the barriers of attendance reduced, and the medium-provided anonymity, she felt comfortable exploring our digital offerings. Once she decided the community was safe, she joined the prayer video chat after worship. And when she heard about Accidental Saints, she decided it was exactly what she had been looking for. It was a place she could bring her concerns, her fears, her hurts, and not have them 'solved.' She could have others listen to her struggles without trying to fix her. It became a place for her to bounce around ideas with others who were questioning their own faith, people who would allow her to have her doubts and process them in her own time. Instead of having to leave the church altogether, she was provided a space of support.

If we had treated our digital book group as less real than an in-person gathering, there would have been no way to allow for the closeness and community that emerged in those two years together. I have another friend who is known to wax philosophical about the hyperreality and potential of online relationships. If asked, he will begin by telling anyone who will listen that he met his wife on Christian Mingle. He details the slow progression of messaging through the app, then texting one another, and finally meeting in person. They have now been married over six years and have an infant daughter. He will talk about how they frequently Facetime as a family. Then he will point out how his mother met her best friend on a message board in the nineties. They have been close for almost thirty years and have never met in person, but her kids call the best friend, "Aunt Trudy." After he's done sharing these stories, he will remind everyone that the dating app, text messaging, video chat, and message boards are all virtual, but they are no less real. He tells this story to show how real our digital lives truly are. There is no IRL (in real life) versus online. It is all real life. These digital interactions are as real as we let them be.

3. Digital Community Can Be Even More Life-Giving

Digital community can actually be even more life-giving and supportive than in-person community. Recently I was talking to Robert, a young man in my congregation who was annoyed that it took a worldwide pandemic for everyone to notice that digital community is real. He shared that every outcast kid has known their whole life that the only place they could find others like them was on the internet. In cities and neighborhoods that might not have an LGBTQ center, the internet has provided a sense of community for kids to support one another for years. I didn't realize this same digital support would translate to my ministry, and not only to my parishioners, but also to me.

The support I received through this season was powerful and moving. I was brought up in a traditional model of ministry. The pastor is meant to minister *to* the people, never the other way around. However, not only did this Accidental Saints group remain the centerpiece of my church's outreach throughout the lockdown and beyond, but it also became a place for me to gather insights and ideas for ministry. It became a time for me to workshop and develop ideas for making online ministry better and more effective. Most people who came to the group were also a part of online worship. They had heard my sermon the day before. Our small group was a place where I felt safe to ask how things were going with my preaching and teaching. I could ask if they understood what I was trying to say. I could ask if they agreed or if they thought I was way off base. When I was struggling with a pattern of rapidly declining engagement on Sunday mornings and lower participation throughout the week, I could ask this group what I could do better and know that I was hearing the truth.

It was distressing to be the pastor in charge in early March 2020 and having to make the decision to close our church to in-person worship. It was one of the most difficult moments of my professional life. I had only been a lead pastor for a couple of years and was leading a congregation that was incredibly diverse in terms of beliefs, politics, education, and socio-economic status. There was no way to know how they would react to the closure. Before that moment, I had felt invincible in my ministry in that church. Most of what I had done as a new, young pastor had been well received and was often met with encouragement. We were the first congregation in our area to announce a closure and many people had put their heads in the sand, hoping the situation would blow over. One decision could impact the rest of my ministry.

Then it got worse. When we began offering online worship that first Sunday, the video was so awful. The first recordings were done with my phone attached to a handheld tripod, which was then duct taped to a cookie sheet (literally) so the person holding the camera would have makeshift image stabilization. It wasn't good at all, but it was 'good enough' to meet our goals of the moment. That said, the result was incredibly rough. The video was shaky, the audio was inconsistent and difficult to understand, and the overall presentation was unprofessional. Though I never let anyone know outside of my own head, my goal was simple: I wanted to hold the space, to keep Sabbath worship in the lives of my parishioners, until we inevitably moved back to in-person worship, and we could leave this digital hellscape behind forever. However, because my goal was so meager, it meant that the results of our ad hoc, low-quality recordings were not very good.

The pressure from having to create an online worship experience each week took an incredible emotional toll on me. I would end worship each Sunday, walk home from church, and feel absolutely wrecked because I was so embarrassed. I was holding myself to a standard I could not hope to reach. I would try to remind myself each Monday morning that we would be back in person soon and I could stop thinking about how poorly I was performing at my job. I would tell myself that we would certainly return to in-person worship by Easter. But when Easter came and went, I reminded myself that we would be back by May. But then May came and went. Then it was Pentecost and I could no longer deny that it would be a while before my much-hoped-for return would come. But when things felt like they were falling apart, I was met with love and support and prayer. Without a group like Accidental Saints, it would have been even more challenging to stay sane through that season.

The group became a time of sharing and prayer, not just for me, but for everyone. One day Lee, a retired executive, shared that the pastor's wife from the church he grew up in wanted to be remembered in our prayers. A couple of weeks later, he mentioned that she was very interested in the book we were reading. Then one day she showed up in the Zoom grid. It was in this way that we met Ilene, a ninety-plus-year-old who was stuck in a nursing facility. Lee had been calling her regularly to make sure she was doing okay and almost always talked about being a part of Accidental Saints. She was in a nursing home in Florida and in the process of dying. She was very ill and often joined us on her iPad from her bed. She struggled with the technology, but she read every book with the voracious appetite of a lifelong reader. She would come to the group whenever she did not have an appointment to see the doctor. When she would miss or make a slight scene because of her struggles with technology, Lee would remind us that these couple of hours were the highlight of her week. A group that began as a time of intellectual, theological discussion eventually progressed to also be a time of spiritual practice and prayer. As we talked and prayed, we could brainstorm how to keep everyone connected, even when we couldn't be together. We began to get into the habit of mentioning people we hadn't heard from lately.

"You know, I haven't heard from Joan," Kate might say.

"Nancy has two young kids at home and a high-power career. I wonder how she is holding up," another might offer. We would then lift that person up in prayer together. Then one day, Belle, a retired city planner, contacted me to complain. "It's all well and good for us to pray for these people" she said. "I mean, I know it's important, but shouldn't we also be checking on them too?" My first instinct was to get defensive. In those first few months of the pandemic lockdown, I was working harder than I ever had, trying to learn video editing and best practices for social media and communication, while also needing to write sermons and provide pastoral care. To say that I was feeling burned out would be an understatement. Instead, I took a breath and asked, "Is that something you would like to do?" It was at that moment that our group, through Belle's leadership, also became a centerpiece of congregational care.

Moments of check-in became moments of grace, a time for people to learn how they could help or be helped. The Holy Spirit moved among us and enlightened and inspired us to be change agents and caretakers. We would begin each session like the eighteenth-century English priest and founder of the Methodist movement, John Wesley. He opened his small-group meetings with the question, "How is it with your soul?" It is an acknowledgement that you are more than how you are doing today. During the pandemic lockdown, people would join a video chat with me and ask, "So, how are ya?" And I would reply with a glib, "Is *anyone* okay?" However, when this group would ask me, "How is it with your soul?" I would be much more open to share the truth of what was going on in my life. It is a deeper question that makes it possible to tell the story of what God is doing in our lives. It makes possible authentic sharing and prayerful reflection. In this way, digital community can truly be even more life-giving than in-person community.

Best Practices

It is quite the coincidence that Accidental Saints was founded by accident. It wasn't planned in the least. I had not intended to continue completely online beyond the pandemic. The online component was only meant to keep us going until we could head back to the coffee shop. Sometimes I wish I could go back in time to the moment Madeline joined because, in retrospect, I see a significant mistake. If I could do it again, I would have created a sustainable online ministry by separating the online worship, video chat prayer gatherings, and even the book gathering to make them distinct digital satellite congregations. I would still see myself as the pastor of the brick-and-mortar church, but like many large churches, I would have smaller congregations online that might never make their way to the actual building. They may not even interact with each other online. By seeing these digital spaces as distinct congregations, I would have been able create communities that would be sustainable long after COVID-19.

Unfortunately, I learned this too late. Just four years into serving my congregation in San Diego, I was transferred by the bishop from San Diego to Orange County. Many members of this digital community were not connected to my congregation in San Diego; they were connected to me and to the other participants. By leaving the digital space behind, I caused a domino effect and left the people with no connection to the congregation in the care of a pastor they'd never met. They had no reason to stick around to meet that new pastor and most moved on. To make matters worse, I later heard the group lost track of Ilene and she passed away amidst the shuffle. She died no longer being a part of the group. In hindsight, I would have allowed the digital ministry to remain distinct and separate from the broader congregation. That way, when I moved, I could have maintained that community as a distinct parish that could accompany me into the foreseeable future.

Even with all the obvious failures, the digital space provided many huge bonuses that I would never give back. One of the most surprising gifts was that authors were often willing to come and speak and lead discussions on Zoom. More than once I reached out and they were delighted to be invited. Seldom did their participation even come with a cost. Even when they asked for an honorarium, because there were no travel expenses, the cost was negligible. There is no way a church like mine could have ever afforded to bring these authors to speak in a pre-pandemic world.

I still remember when an open and relational theologian came for a question-and-answer session on Zoom. He was describing the God of his theological system and how this version of God helped people who had been abused or who were victims of trauma to find their way back to the divine. It was a brilliant exposition of a divine presence who will never force its will upon us. It was poetic and beautiful and answered the questions that many of our deconstructing participants were asking. But then Mike, a nonprofit executive in his early fifties, who often used the language of an all-powerful and almighty God, unmuted his mic and said, "I'm sorry if that's your God, your God isn't good enough." I would venture this theologian had not received such a casual and pointed criticism before. In a world where brick-and-mortar locations are the only thing that matters, these two would have never met. Technology and an openness to true digital community allowed us to have unforgettable interactions with people we would never have had a chance to engage.

Conclusion

Recognizing that the cost of admission for creating digital community is low and allows pastors to increase church participation beyond the people who are currently a part of their congregation, it seems like a no-brainer for almost every small church pastor to seek and find their digital audience. Most importantly, we cannot forget that by building a digital community, we provide an opportunity for people to experience the divine in their lives. By taking the time to share God digitally, it creates a space in which they can know that God is present and loves them just as they are.

I only wish that it wouldn't have taken a worldwide pandemic for us to realize the power of digital community building. The phone call with my friend ended like this. "So, you think none of this real? You haven't had any Spirit-filled experiences in online spaces?" He repeated that none of it felt as real and said he thought it was at best a poor substitute for in-person activities. Of course, with all I had learned in the previous months, I wholeheartedly disagreed. We are close friends, so we continued arguing for a while, but hung up the phone without resolving anything. With that, I was content to move on because I was confident in the grace that I had experienced with this mismatched group of folks devoted to following Christ and loving and caring for one another. Knowing that grace, I couldn't help but move forward into the emerging world of digital ministry.

Rev. Matt Hambrick (he/him) is the Lead Pastor at Costa Mesa First United Methodist. He is known for engaging and thought-provoking sermons and for riding his pink skateboard around the church. Matt started pastoring after studying philosophy and religion at Point Loma Nazarene University and Claremont School of Theology. At seminary, Matt found his passion for ministry, specifically for gathering people who have been traditionally left out by the mainstream church. His favorite part of ministry is hearing the stories of God's redemptive love and grace told uniquely by every person he meets. You can follow him on Instagram at @revhambrick

3

A Full Ministry from an Empty Building

Rev. Dr. Caleb J. Lines

Imagine a church building with a completely full sanctuary and multiple worship services. Think of a church education building where each room is bustling with children of all ages. Picture a parking lot filled with cars on Sunday morning. Have you ever experienced a church like this? Perhaps you have. In fact, I've heard about this church from older members of every congregation that I have ever served as they recall the "glory days." But if I'm being honest, I can't really relate to their rose-colored memories of the past, because they are describing a church that I've never known. As an "elder millennial"—which describes those of us who were born in the mid-1980s—and as a lifelong mainline Protestant, I have only ever known a dying church. Luckily, with the decline I have grown much more confident that God is not dependent upon the institutional church; God would be in our midst even if every sanctuary were completely empty on Sunday mornings. But what do we do with those now mostly empty buildings? I believe those empty buildings can help us to rethink church finances in a digital age to ensure full ministries.

Understanding the Problem

As Phyllis Tickle told us well over a decade ago, the church has been going through what she calls the "Great Emergence" for the past several decades. She argues that every five hundred years or so the church has a great rummage sale, of sorts, and does away with beliefs and practices that are no longer relevant.[1] While it's somewhat comforting to know that a shake-up in the religious status quo has happened several times throughout Christian history, that doesn't make it any less disorienting, particularly for those in church leadership. Clergy are scrambling to lead in a space where the ground is constantly shifting under our feet.

As we've come to terms with the fact that the church we've known will not exist in the future, we've recognized that some of the decline has been self-imposed (like ostracizing entire groups of people, i.e. the LGBTQIA+ community) and some of it has had to do with the changes in the ways that we relate to one another. The changing nature of human relationships is something that has been a subtle, but substantial change. Over the past few decades, relationality has shifted as we began to rely less on physical community and much more on digital community. This change has really sped up over the past decade or so. As usual, the church has been notoriously slow to catch on to what has become commonplace in all other spheres of life.

While the rest of the world had quickly embraced all things digital, many churches approached the digital world with caution, sometimes dismissing it completely . . . until the COVID-19 pandemic proved once and for all that digital content creation was here to stay. Churches that embraced digital media during the pandemic likely found that it could actually lead to church growth, if approached intentionally.[2] While many churches may hope to one day return to congregational life as it once was, that doesn't

1. Phyllis Tickle, *The Great Emergence: How Christianity is Changing and Why* (Grand Rapids: Baker, 2008).

2. I write more about why this is true in my recent book: Caleb J. Lines, *The Great Digital Commission: Embracing Social Media for Church Growth and Transformation* (Eugene: Cascade, 2021).

seem plausible. This means that churches must change the ways that they think about finances in a digital world.

Understanding Finances in a New Age

While we know that the church is changing, that doesn't mean that congregations that are declining can't still have an enormous impact on the lives of congregants and the communities in which the physical buildings are located. But how can churches with large physical properties continue to function in a digital world? There's much to say about ways that donor giving can become even stronger with an increased digital presence, particularly if you use social media to highlight the unique ministries that your congregation is doing. In fact, doing so effectively can often lead to people far away from your physical location financially contributing to your ministry. We've seen this at the congregation I serve as we've increased our own social media presence. However, at the end of the day, no matter how good your digital ministry is, for many established congregations, donor giving is not going to be enough to continue doing ministry.

It's time for church leaders to help their congregations find inventive ways to diversify their income streams in order to survive. With some creativity, congregations can not only survive, but can thrive even as the ground beneath us shifts in the church. While there are several ways to think about diversifying income streams, one of the glaring resources that churches have at their disposal is their building. Churches need to take a long, hard look at their physical space. I assume that many of us do not recognize the church that I described at the beginning of the chapter with a completely full sanctuary, multiple services, education classrooms bustling with children, and a packed parking lot. Instead, many of our buildings sit empty for most of the week and parking lots are often wasted space. The physical properties that we inhabit were built for a different time with a completely different model of ministry. Even if your church happens to be growing, it's unlikely that you will need the church building for a 1950s model of church. The congregation that

I serve has doubled in size since I began, but our model of ministry doesn't necessitate an entire building filled with classrooms.

Think about your church property. For the most part, other than the church offices, the building is likely designed to meet needs on Sunday morning, but most of the rooms likely sit vacant during the week. Most churches were designed to be used for a couple of hours once a week. If your church is like most churches, there has probably been a great deal of deferred maintenance, as well. This means that as things break, the building can become a great liability. For instance, a few years ago we had a gas leak that cost upwards of $30,000 to repair, then a water leak that cost another $30,000. At one of the churches I previously served, we could not get the sanctuary to stop leaking, no matter how much money we threw at it! Every church that I've ever served has grossly underestimated maintenance costs and the budget has been thrown off each year by costly surprises. Here's the point: church buildings cost a great deal of money to sit unused most of the week. Many of us feel like we are living in service to our buildings rather than our buildings serving us. A mentor once told me that he only spent about five hours of each week actually doing anything theological . . . the rest of his time was spent dealing with issues that arose from being in an old building. When I started in ministry, I quickly understood what he meant!

While buildings can certainly be a liability, our buildings can serve us once again instead of us serving them. We can leverage our buildings to enhance our congregations and our communities, while generating income. To help demonstrate what I mean, I'd like to share the story of how the congregation I serve has been transforming its physical space into an income generator.

A Story of Transformation

I serve a mainline Protestant congregation in San Diego affiliated with two denominations that continue to experience rapid membership decline. A few years ago, we recognized that even though our congregation was bucking the current trend of decreasing membership, we still faced many of the same challenges that most churches are dealing with these days: 1) aging buildings and 2) inadequate finances to thrive in ministry. We had a tough reality to face. Even though we were growing, given trends and cultural shifts meant that we would not be able to continue ministry in the future; we were going to run out of money. We needed to rethink the way that we did ministry if we were going to continue to exist. Luckily, the church had an endowment that allowed us the most precious resource of all: time. We needed time to discern who we were and who we wanted to be in the future. We decided to do something unheard of . . . we dedicated $150,000 for the year to be used exclusively for creative ministry. A variety of life-giving projects came out of that, but one of the most significant was a master plan for rethinking our property. Our facility was built "California style" meaning that it consists of four separate non-connected buildings. The newest of these buildings was built in the mid-sixties. Needless to say, all four buildings were aging, and upkeep was becoming a significant cost.

We were already further along in leveraging our building for income than many congregations. We had converted the bottom floor of our two-story education building into a preschool. This preschool was helping to provide affordable childcare to a community that desperately needed it. We rented out our sanctuary to musical groups that needed a rehearsal space or a concert venue. We rented out several rooms on the second floor of our education building to nonprofits and recovery groups. All of this helped us to generate income, but honestly, if there were any unexpected building expenses, a good chunk of the money went into building repair because we had deferred maintenance for so long.

We began to realize that even with the additional income that we were receiving from renting space in our building, the model we had for ministry was no longer working. We came up with five different options for how we could proceed:

1. Continue doing ministry the same way that we had been and use our existing endowment until it was gone. If we didn't change anything, even with the growth that we were

experiencing, we knew we would deplete our endowment in the next few years and would likely be forced to close our doors in less than a decade.

2. Cut staff. We were already working with a skeleton staffing structure. The congregation could have gone to a part-time minister and enlisted volunteers to help cover the tasks that were currently being filled by paid staff members, but we knew that this would likely reverse the progress that we'd made over the past few years that had helped the church to grow in membership. The congregation would also have to find another pastor who'd be willing to work part-time, because I was very clear that it wouldn't be me.

3. Sell the property and move. We knew that we were sitting on a multimillion-dollar piece of property, so we could sell it. However, the congregation had a long history of being very active in our community and we realized that if we packed up and moved out of our neighborhood, it would fundamentally change our identity.

4. Better utilize our existing facility for income generation. We had already moved most of our programs out of our education building so that we could rent out the space. After crunching the numbers, we discovered that we could generate almost $100,000/year by renting the remainder of our space to nonprofits. That would go a long way towards addressing our budget deficit, but it would not address parking (we're an urban church and parking is always a problem) or concerns about an aging building. Better utilizing our building would allow us to survive, but not to thrive.

5. We could sell a portion of our land to a housing developer (there's a severe housing shortage in San Diego) and do a building project on the other portion of land that we would retain. This project would be complicated, and it would be a multiyear endeavor that would be built in phases. Once the project was completed, however, we believed that it would

solve many of our existing problems and help us to live into our mission more fully.

The congregation weighed the options and decided to move forward with a sale of half of the property while doing an extensive renovation/rebuild of the other half that we would retain. We decided that if we were going to move forward, we were going to do it with intentionality and we were going to be cognizant of our mission, vision, and core values. To buy ourselves a bit of additional time, we began better utilizing our property by renting out all of our remaining available space so that we were maximizing income generation from our existing building. As we began to make decisions, we always kept our core values at the forefront of our process. Below, I've listed our core values, to help clarify how we made our decisions:

- We are a ***progressive congregation*** that takes the Bible seriously, but not always literally. Doubters are welcome here.

- We are an ***Open & Affirming Congregation*** that welcomes people of all sexual orientations and gender identities into the full life and leadership of the church. We are a proud member of the Disciples LGBTQ+ Alliance, the Open & Affirming Coalition of the United Church of Christ, and were the first Open and Affirming Disciples Congregation in Southern California.

- We are a ***multiracial/multicultural congregation*** that openly welcomes people of all races and ethnicities to help weave the diverse tapestry of our community of faith. We are always striving to be a pro-reconciling/anti-racist congregation.

- We are an ***environmentally conscious congregation*** that cares for God's creation and strives to be good stewards of it.

- We are a ***peace and justice congregation***. We believe that God cares deeply for those who are oppressed and marginalized and make our mission to those in need the center of our ministry.

As we moved forward, we began by thinking about the kind of housing developer with whom wanted to partner. Since our fifth core value was being a congregation that strives for peace and justice, we decided to fully explore affordable housing, knowing that it's a gamble (there's an extensive process of applying for tax credit funds). Luckily, we had sufficient time to partner with an affordable housing developer and let them apply to the state and local government agencies for funds. We knew that if the developer did not receive funds for affordable housing, we would partner with a community-minded developer who was committed to providing middle-income housing with a percentage of units dedicated to affordable housing. We would need to negotiate ground floor space in the apartment building and parking spaces. Once the land was sold, we would replenish our endowment funds that we'd used to stay afloat for the past several years and further invest funds. We began to explore funds with our denominational investment institution and were particularly drawn to investments that were divested from fossil fuels, since being an environmentally conscious congregation was our fourth core value. Interest from the endowment funds would be one sizable alternative income stream.

On the other half of our property—the half that we'd be retaining for church use—we needed to remodel/rebuild structures to produce income and enhance our mission. After extensive work with construction and church consultants, we decided to tear down our social hall and chapel and build a new building which would serve two purposes. First, through a master-planning process, we recognized that our preschool was a priority for the congregation. Since there was and is a childcare shortage in San Diego, affordable childcare was also a justice issue for us and compatible with our core values. We decided to build a new preschool space and to increase the number of students. As previously mentioned, our preschool had already been generating income and had a waiting list, so we felt confident that it was a reliable income stream that could be bolstered. Second, we would build brand new below-market-rent office space to house nonprofits. Before long, nonprofits who were attracted to our vision came onto our campus and temporarily made their home in our education building as they awaited brand new office space. We would house the Gay Men's Chorus (which was compatible with our second core value of being Open & Affirming), a home-building organization (our fifth core value of striving for peace and justice), and a newly formed Climate Hub of five environmental justice nonprofits (our fourth core value of being environmentally conscious). The nonprofits would constitute another alternative income stream and there would be increased opportunities for our congregation to collaborate with organizations that were already doing a lot of the work we wanted to put at the center of our mission.

As the plan clarified, we began to realize that we would have at least four income streams: traditional donor giving, income from sizable endowment funds, tuition from the preschool, and rent from nonprofits with a similar mission. We crunched the numbers and found that this plan allowed us to not only meet current budget needs, but also to expand our staff and programs in the ways that we had been dreaming about for years. Furthermore, we recognized that with some planning, we could likely fund the day-to-day operations of the church—like staff salaries and administrative cost—with the alternative income streams so that donor giving could all go to the ministries of the church where people could see the impact that their gifts were making. People are more likely to give if they can see the direct result of their gifts! This plan ensured that the operations of the church were covered in a stable way and that the ministry of the church could function through the generosity of the congregation.

This story isn't quite a success story yet, as we are currently in the midst of actually building the project! But all is progressing nicely, and our alternative income streams are on track to be in place very soon. The entire process has been transformational for the congregation, as we have become future-focused, which has led to palpable excitement and further membership growth. Our property is now helping us to realize our mission and vision more fully.

Discerning the Path

The exact approach that a congregation takes to better utilize its physical property will, of course, vary based on its individual circumstances, but being willing to be creative is essential. When we were in the initial stages of our project, we had to acknowledge the elephant in the room: the plan sounded good, but it could fail, and the church could close despite our best efforts. We decided that if we were going to close, we would have at least *tried* to prevent it. One of the biggest mistakes that congregations make is that they don't really try new things for fear of losing what they already have. The only way to really create substantive change is to take creative risks. They might fail, but how worse off would the congregation be if you're headed towards closing the physical doors anyway?

We were fortunate that we had an endowment to allow us both time and finances to explore our options, a property that was desirable and held significant land value, and lay leadership that was invested in the future of the church and not stuck in the past. However, even if you do not have these luxuries, creative use of space will likely be essential to explore, particularly as more ministry is done digitally and there is less need for massive physical church structures. By creating a digital sanctuary, you free the physical one to enhance your ministry beyond Sunday morning.

One of the best things that you can do in ministry is to get to know your neighborhood. Who are your neighbors and what are their needs? How do those needs fit in with your own mission/vision as a congregation? Are there ways that you can utilize your building to enhance your ministry, serve your community, and also generate income? I've seen some congregations turn their entire facility into a nonprofit space, where the church is just one of many nonprofits housed in the location. Other churches have negotiated with housing developers who have purchased the entire property but built a new space for a congregation on a small portion of the property . . . the congregation has then built a relationship with those who live in the housing next to them. Some churches might partner with the city to put tiny homes on an oversized parking lot to help address homelessness. Some churches might redesign their worship space to function as an event venue or arts space. Some might partner with a university or other school that needs physical classroom space. Whatever a congregation decides to do with its space, it should be looking for compatible partner organizations. It's true that property value is higher and there is more potential to rent the physical property in urban areas, but with creativity, it can be done in rural locations, as well. Even in more rural communities, perhaps there are opportunities for partnerships with food banks, homeless resource centers, local nonprofits, or area farmers to create a farmer's market. Anything that you can do to ensure that the church space doesn't sit vacant for six days a week will strengthen your ministry.

Partnership is the key to successful ministry, particularly in this age of seismic shifts in the ways that churches operate. Just remember that whoever shares your space needs to be a nonprofit (or else you could end up paying property tax on the space used by a for-profit business) and that their mission is compatible with your congregation's values. One thing that you'll likely discover is that in addition to the income generated from creative use of your congregation's space, there will likely be people from those other organizations who will appreciate the work of the church and may consider your congregation to be their church home. Before we began work on our building project, we discovered that we had over a thousand people on our campus every week (and that doesn't include anyone who was there for worship or our preschool!). Creating a welcoming and hospitable environment where a church is clearly serving the community can be a powerful statement about how the church is (or should be) about much more than what you do in a single room on Sunday mornings.

Moving Forward

As you move forward with the exploration of changes to your physical sanctuary, the digital sanctuary ought to be at the forefront of you mind. When partnerships are developed with other organizations, amplify these partnerships with posts on social media. These posts show the community that you are invested in making the world a better place and that you practice what you preach. If you can show theologically why you support the work of another organization, even better. When you utilize social media to highlight partnerships, you connect the physical space with the digital world.

The spaces that we retrain for church use ought to be designed with a digital audience in mind. I believe that it's important for congregations to continue to create physical community where possible, because relationships often form organically in physical communities differently than they do online (sitting down next to someone in church and chatting for a few minutes before the service begins, for instance). However, we know that the digital world is here to stay, and quality audio/video equipment needs to installed in the worship space and in meeting rooms/classrooms so that people have a hybrid option. Following the COVID-19 pandemic, many churches will likely want to kill the tap on digital options to force people back to the physical buildings, but that's a mistake. Embracing hybrid options and even developing a digital worshiping community in addition to your physical community will likely help your congregation to grow and will give you more bodies to fill roles in your congregation.

Conclusion

The digital sanctuary is here to stay and for the most part, it's a good thing. Existing congregations are often stuck with a physical sanctuary not equipped for an increasingly digital world. The building doesn't have to be a liability, though. With some intentionality, planning, and creativity, it can become a tool to serve your congregation's financial needs in an age where donor giving is likely to continue to decline. Embrace the digital sanctuary and transform your empty church building into a full ministry!

Rev. Dr. Caleb J. Lines (he/him) is an ordained minister with standing in the Christian Church (Disciples of Christ) and the United Church of Christ. He currently serves as the senior minister of University Christian Church in San Diego, the co-executive director of ProgressiveChristianity.org, and co-host of the podcast "The Moonshine Jesus Show." Caleb is the author of *The Great Digital Commission: Embracing Social Media for Church Growth and Transformation* (Cascade Books, 2021), which quickly reached #1 on Amazon's New Releases for Church Growth and was awarded a Silver Medal Illumination Book Award in Ministry/Mission. Visit his website at calebjlines.com.

4

Reimagining Participation and Inclusion

Rev. Rich Tafel

When the COVID pandemic swept the world in 2020 we all realized at some level an "old normal" was passing away. Church leaders could not comprehend the seismic shifts that would rock the church. The coming "digital church" leaves behind what we've imagined "church" to be. The shift to a digital church marks the moment when the church literally left the building and allowed all of us to reimagine the reality of church as a spiritual community.

One of the key challenges for the emerging digital church is to reimagine the new possibilities for participation and inclusion as well as an opportunity to heal divides from the old way we embodied "church".

A friend described our church, the Church of the Holy City in Washington, DC as a "rescue church." I'd never heard that phrase and I know he meant it as a compliment. Six years ago I took over as part-time pastor to a beautiful, historic church building that needed major renovations. It had five members left, and their average age was seventy-two. Growing an urban church against the tide of secularism is tough enough. Today, we are still small, but our membership now ranges in age from twenty-eight to ninety-four; we are racially, theologically, geographically, and gender-diverse. Our evolution to become a "digital church" made much of our growth possible.

Our entire mission as a church is to help people on their own spiritual path. Our entire challenge is becoming more inclusive and more participatory. The story of the COVID pandemic forced us kicking and screaming into the digital age and the struggles of this era have turned into an incredible unexpected blessing. In our tradition, Swedenborgianism, we believe that all evil events are ultimately bent by God toward good—the digital church is one of the goods that has emerged from the horrors of this pandemic.

As the church has left the building and a digital congregation from around the world has been growing, I've reflected upon a few lessons I've learned about participation and inclusion in a digital church space that I hope are helpful to other communities navigating the emerging digital age of church.

Lesson 1: The Digital Church Must Be Participatory and Inclusive

The first lesson of the digital church is that it will be participatory and inclusive, or it won't exist at all. In this moment, not only has technology evolved, but also our spirituality which invites us to embrace the radically inclusive message of Jesus.

Coming into the pandemic, our church was quickly moving from a top-down model of leadership to a congregational model where the whole group co-creates and collaborates. We knew the days had passed when older white men with gray hair pontificate from the pulpit and tell their parishioners what to do. (I say that as an older white man with gray hair.) The rising postmodern, post-church generation[1] simply won't buy what church is selling if they can't participate, question, doubt, and challenge what they hear.

1. "The post-modern worldview believes that we each have our own truth and is suspicious of any capital "T" truth. Though spiritual seekers, they are "post-church" in how they grew up hearing about it as a judgmental and hypocritical institution and have written off the church as their grandparents knew it."

In our tradition, we believe that one can only come to true faith through doubt, which invites us to reimagine church as a place where congregants can seek moral and spiritual guidance from our tradition, but then are invited to question what they hear until they uncover the truth for themselves.

Like congregations across the world, my congregation at Church of the Holy City in Washington, DC experienced a crisis as we tried to plan for service on Sunday of March 14, 2020. Word of the spread of the coronavirus led our leadership into a frantic series of emails deciding whether to stay open or close.

Elders in the group all suggested we remain open. "We've been through worse, you know." While my younger members felt what was coming was uniquely serious and to be responsible, we needed to cancel services. Against the wishes of my church elders, I decided as pastor that we'd cancel in-person services. After sharing my decision with our community, one church elder wrote back in support, "Dear Rich, thank you for agonizing over this issue to such length. I hope you'll get some rest now."

With that decision we scrambled to find a conference call number to gather our community on and sent out our third conflicting announcement to our newsletter list. Little did we know the extent of the coming pandemic and how life in our church would never be the same.

When I took over Church of the Holy City as their part-time pastor, I was already working in a position at a social impact investment advisory organization and had developed a coaching practice. When I started, we had four members in a sanctuary that sat two hundred. My first suggestion was that rather than lament the empty pews, we should imagine the sanctuary as a TV studio and broadcast for others beyond our four walls with our in-person congregation serving as the "live audience". At the time, church members didn't really like the idea, but a version of this would be kicked around in many board meetings for the next four years. We never moved to do it . . . until the pandemic forced us to reimagine.

When coronavirus hit, and we found ourselves a digital congregation overnight. We had to rethink participation and inclusion in some dramatic ways. As we bounced from one teleconference service to another, we saw so many others land on using the video conferencing program Zoom. I'd become very comfortable with being online, having used Skype for my coaching with clients around the world for over two decades. Zoom wasn't that hard for me to shift to; however, it was a huge shift for our elder members. Our younger tech savvy members had watched Zoom events get hacked and so they suggested that we keep the Zoom sign-in codes different each week and accessible only by our church newsletter.

The future of church is going to be digital; the question is how do we harness this for good.

Lesson 2: Digital Church Must Overcome the Barriers to Technology

This led to our second lesson concerning the participation challenge of the digital age. Technology can be radically inclusive, but it can also be a barrier to participation. Technology can be great to connect people but can be an incredible burden for older members who are unfamiliar with the constantly emerging new technology. As the service would start each week elder members would call anxiously, saying that they couldn't get in because of the lack of owning a computer or simply not understanding the basics of getting online. It broke my heart as I tried to juggle their calls with the others showing up in the Zoom room to begin our worship gathering.

For participation to work, there needed to be hand-holding and training from the church community. Two angels emerged in our community: Annabel Park and Kateryna Pyatybratova, both tech-savvy leaders, both immigrants who knew the pain of being outside the conversation. They divided up members and coached them into the room each week a half hour before we began until all of our members felt comfortable logging on to Zoom on their own.

The first level of participation is *access*. Some in our community who suffered from challenging home situations and financial challenges stopped trying to join using their phones which proved to be overly burdensome. Our community brainstormed about donating old computers and paying for online access, but the barrier just became too much and while they continued participating through pastoral check-ins, we initially failed to find an easy way for them to succeed in connecting to our weekly gatherings.

We also eventually agreed to always use the same Zoom sign in to ensure older members didn't have to fumble with new codes or links each week. I jokingly explained to our small group that if we got crashed it would add excitement to our gatherings and we'd handle it together as a community.

"Another great advantage of digital worship is that we are re-using sermons to create podcasts on their spiritual resilience. The downside is that some younger members only listen to the podcast versions and don't attend church. The upside is that our message is getting out to serve younger listeners on their terms."

Some of the members of the church who lacked proper technology to participate were "adopted" by some other members, who invited them into their homes to participate in the service and then shared a meal with them. Simply removing the digital barriers consumed our early efforts for participation—but it was essential to ensure that as many people could be included in our community as possible.

As the pandemic rolled on, participation reached record numbers initially. People were very afraid, and fear leads people to go to faith communities for answers. We had numerous first-time visitors. Slowly, our elder loyal crowd got the hang of Zoom, muting themselves and enjoying the ease of connection from their comfortable chairs at home.

But then a new trend developed.

My twenty-something members told me that they were "Zoomed out." They were now spending hours at work with clients each day on screens. The idea of getting back on-screen for church was too much. Some surprised me by saying for them church was being in the sanctuary and being online didn't cut it. Just as the elder participation ticked up the younger participation dropped. Though they've participated in one-on-one pastoral calls, some have never returned to worship.

The digital church will need to continually find new strategies to overcome barriers to access to various demographics.

Lesson 3: Creating a Digital Holy Space Requires Reimagining Tradition

The digital worship service is an incredible way to invite your community into the process of reimagining their traditions. In our church, once people adapted to life online, we sought ways to create a holy space without the benefit of each of us being able to gather in our physical sanctuary. Each week I'd broadcast our service from within our sanctuary, lighting a candle and opening the Bible in our physical sanctuary as I invited others to do so in their homes. People really got into creating a sacred space in their homes and began sending in photos of their home altars created for worship. After this introductory ritual, I added a brief time of meditative, deep breathing as attendees were invited to shake off the world they'd come from and enter a sacred time.

In our community like in many others, attempts to incorporate music into the virtual service were difficult, but members insisted that we find a way to start with music. As a way to increase participation and inclusion, we started a new tradition where we invited members to make suggestions for opening songs and share why the song was meaningful to them, opening up an incredible opportunity for vulnerability and sharing together. Week by week, a new liturgy began to evolve based on the congregation's needs and input.

The lesson I learned in this season that I've held to as our ministry has continued to evolve is that co-creating a worship experience with members has true power to transform a worship experience. At the same time, in order to stay grounded within our tradition in the midst of innovation and collaboration, the minister must provide reminders for why we do what we do.

The liturgy I inherited at my church sounded like an Anglican service from the 1600s. The service today is infused with input from attendees. Facilitating the discussion of what people want creates incredible opportunities for participation and a sense of belonging within the community. Members now read, pick the music, read the Scriptures and insights from Swedenborg (whose writings are the source of our denomination's distinctive spiritual outlook), offer prayers, and participate in a discussion of the sermon. The entire service is now interactive.

This radically inclusive, participant-centered model doesn't mean anarchy. At the same time, it allows our members to question, critique, and learn about our tradition. Some of my younger members have asked if we could skip the invocation and confession because it doesn't fit their theological paradigm. Others questioned why we did certain readings. As one person put it, "I like your message—it's like the *Radio Hour* podcast. I learn a lot. I just get bored with the rest of the stuff."

These questions and comments give the pastor an opportunity to educate. "Here's why we invoke God's presence." "Here's why we confess our sins." "Here's why we ground teachings in the Word and read it." Each Sunday presents a new opportunity for the minister to explain our tradition and practices, helping the community to grow deeper in their experience.

As the digital service took off, we gained attendees from all over the US and sometimes even the UK. As the church doors were closed due to COVID, something else happened. Many of our members left living in the city of DC for cheaper housing elsewhere. Ironically, despite these losses, our church grew thanks to being online. Had we simply been in person, it is hard to say if such growth would have ever happened.

Tradition is valuable and much of it serves an important purpose. It seems clear that digital churches will need to decide what's valuable and what can be left behind, while also educating a rising generation unfamiliar with tradition of the value and reasons for keeping it.

This is also a time to develop new traditions. To further encourage participation, I suggested people come as they are—no need to dress up or present themselves in any way to engage in worship. We scheduled our service for 5 PM Eastern Time which allows for West Coast participants. While many religious services ask you to turn on your camera to participate, we asked people only do what feels comfortable—leave it off if you are in sweatpants, or cooking, or driving. Just come in a way that works for you. In addition, we also tell people that they can leave early if needed—just put a note in the chat. We worked to create an atmosphere of no shame or fear, but complete transparency and authenticity.

Gradually, our digital service evolved to include music, welcome, the word, a candle, a meditative breath, and then the liturgy. Creating a stable container is important not just to make people comfortable, but also to help them expand their minds. Creating a space that allows for the true diversity of ideas is a real opportunity in the digital church.

Lesson 4: Providing a Safe Place to Share

How do you encourage diverse participation when you have a truly diverse congregation?

Before the pandemic, I'd become convinced that the old model of the educated minister preaching down to the sheep in the congregation was a dying model. My church is in the heart of Washington, DC and my younger members are post-church and postmodern. They have little regard for authority, church institutions, or ministers.

When I asked them what's the biggest challenge for them to come to church originally, they simply said, "church."

Priests, they shared with me, were hypocrites who were involved in embezzlement and sexual abuse scandals. A common question at DC social events for me is, "You seem really smart, how did you end up becoming a minister?" For there to be participation and inclusion in church, we must send clear signals of welcome. I have never had a potential new member ask me my views of the Trinity, but almost all have asked what our position is on ordaining women, dealing with racism, or welcoming the LGBTQ+ community.

Long before COVID, I would encourage participants to ask the hard questions. I have training as a facilitator which has proved helpful. Slowly but surely, our discussion time became as valuable, if not more valuable, than the liturgy. In my small congregation we have incredible diversity of sexuality, gender, and race. Our oldest member is ninety-four; our youngest, twenty-five. One half of our members are immigrants. We're one of the few churches I know of with registered Republicans, Democrats, and Socialists.

We're also theologically diverse. Only three members grew up in our denomination, Swedenborgian, which is a version of Christian mysticism. Most over forty grew up in traditional churches with hymns and have knowledge of the Bible. Our under-forty crowd has, for the most part, no deep understanding of Christian tradition. This diversity is an essential part of our tradition and an inescapable reality in our increasingly pluralistic society.

Most of the great divides in churches are ideological—many of us want to go to hear sermons that correspond to our political and theological views. In our community, we've intentionally explored the idea of bridging the divides in ideology.

This has looked like inviting attendees to ask questions that later became sermon topics. Next, we went deeper and asked attendees for sermon topics they thought ministers would be afraid to preach on. This digging deeper brought out requests for sermons on abortion, transgender rights, racism, gay rights, and use of the military. Members wanted to know how to view civic life through a spiritual lens. Each sermon offers the pastor's perspective after also attempting to share other views in a fair manner. Then comes the discussion. As much as possible, we create a space that values the minority perspective. In a city with few Republicans and fewer Trump supporters, we often came back to trying to understand the viewpoints of those not in the room. "Another example of the power of digital sanctuary came at the outbreak of the war against Ukraine. Some 70 people with five identified faith leaders joined us on Zoom to pray together for peace."

In addition to Sunday worship, we used technology to co-host a discussion with South Korea's leading Buddhist monk with Q&A

broadcast to Korea and hosted a discussion about Christian and Muslim mysticism with the Rumi Forum. Our church president and I even attempted a podcast, trying to discuss election events from a spiritual perspective. Creating space for a diversity of opinions and meaningful discussion became the heartbeat of church service during the pandemic. "Another excellent example of inclusion through digital sanctuary was the new programs I taught outside Sunday worship. My background is in impact investing. I led a course on Spiritual Entrepreneurship that helped launch a new business in Washington DC that trains young high school graduates struggling to get into the workforce strategies to land a job. Their pilot in DC was so successful that other states now want the program. All of this was done online."

During the pandemic we lost our church president to cancer that went untreated during the lockdown. In an interview in her final days, she was asked what the mission of the church should be going forward, and with a barely audible voice she said "to be a place where people can share their views without fear." The digital church gives us opportunities to get out of our ideological bubbles and hear perspectives that we don't otherwise get to hear. The church has become a place where we can practice listening and learning from those who see the world differently, and responding with humility and curiosity.

Participation Lesson 5: The Church Has Left the Building

Our little community is now using what we learned about being the national church of our denomination to rethink our building use and imagine what might or might not serve us better in the future. These big decisions we face are both frightening and exhilarating as the very definition of what it means to be a church is redefined. When we asked a group of younger leaders what they'd imagine for the future of our church they began to dream about innovative new ventures such as creating "Holy City Media" featuring more podcasts and other avenues embracing a technical future, as well as the creation of retreat centers and spiritual and social training locations.Our "safe space/sanctuary" transitioned into "safe cyberspace.

Swedenborg, a Christian mystic and the inspiration for the creation of our denomination, described a visionary experience he had about the emergence of a spiritual world in the future where we can simply be with others through our thoughts. In other words, we will no longer have to be physically present to actually be with someone. Looking through this lens of mysticism, the evolving digital age means we can be in the sacred presence of others no matter how far away. Technology is changing our world dramatically, and we can either adapt or be left behind. One of my most recent sermons was on the intersection of spirituality and AI. During the dialogue, I used Chat GPT to answer questions, which was really fun and intriguing. It also addressed a core issue every faith community will face is the impact of AI on spirituality. My conclusion is it will be a net winner for spiritual communities.

In this respect, the digital church is truly a piece of heaven coming to us on earth. It holds incredible opportunities while it also creates new challenges. People still need hugs and physical connection as our loneliness epidemic grows. The question we must wrestle with is how we mix digital church with in-person retreats, events, and worship marks the exciting challenge of new forms of participation in church. None of us knew in March 2020 we'd be closing our doors only to open incredibly new forms of ministry. By building a community that values participation and inclusion, all churches can reimagine church for the digital age.

Rev. Rich Tafel (he/him) is the pastor of the Church of the Holy City in Washington, DC. Tafel has served for eight years on the governing board of the National Council of Churches representing the Swedenborgian Church of North America and currently serves as a Senior Fellow at George Washington University's Center for Excellence in Leadership. Tafel is the founder of Log Cabin Republicans and author of *Party Crasher* (1999, Simon & Schuster).

5

Rethinking Pastoral Care in Digital Ministry

Rev. Paul Swearengin

For years I sat in pastors' meetings listening to leaders bemoan an inability to "get the church people out of the church building." Then, along comes a pandemic and the government kicks people out for us. Rather than seeing the opportunity, however, we capitulate to the squawking and squealing of those very same people demanding their way back into the building. The COVID lockdown shouldn't have been a time of protest, but should have been seen as an exciting opportunity to seek out something new. A new harvest field of "church" in the digital space. I'm starting to share this mantra so often, I now feel like the prophet Isaiah saying: "a new thing springs up in the desert; do you not perceive it?"

People Seeking Transformation in the Digital Faith Space

By the end of my time leading a semi-traditional, charismatic, nondenominational, Protestant church, I was finding the work unfulfilling. I watched in wonder as people listened to my Bible teaching each Sunday and left almost completely unchanged. I've concluded churchgoers have become passive consumers, rather than radical agents of change—looking for a Romans 12:2 transformation so they can transform the world around them. I'm finding greater satisfaction in providing "pastoral care" to those who find me in the digital world.

Online I am "Pastor Paul," emotional and spiritual well-being coach. Those who seek out my help aren't coming for extravagant light show worship times, coffee klatches, and free babysitting in exchange for being forced to listen to a sermon. They come actively looking for someone with gifts to impact their actions and their lives.

In the online faith space, many have left their church communities behind and are finding each other in a community called "deconstructionists." Some pastors disparage this group as people "running from God," but I've found quite the opposite. A people no longer moored to the dogma and indoctrination of their youth are able to fully explore the abundant life promised by the Bible. I find them to be seeking God with all their heart. Also, here's a wonderful little secret: people are willing to pay for this care. And the overhead of doing so is a nano-fraction of the church in a building!

Let's not panic over the shrinking attendance numbers in our churches, but rather embrace the opportunity at hand: A huge harvest field in the digital faith space. There are people out there looking for gifted pastors. Can we be there for them?

What Does the New Thing Look Like?

A pastor friend said to me "we do this deconstruction thing every twenty-five years." He finished with this admonishment:

"If you're in the middle of deconstructing, you better have a plan for reconstructing something else." Isn't it interesting that we continually try this tweak-the-church approach, rather than recognizing a generational passing is at hand? That's why we keep rebuilding what we've always known—about every quarter century.

I see the millennials and Gen Z carrying a new spirituality that may not look like our fathers' Christianity. Yet, it often looks more like Christ than the church system of my lifetime. Rather than another tweak, I believe we can be willing to let go of traditions, dogma, and theological minutiae in order to bless things that look different. To cultivate this next-gen spirituality, we must install new models of delivering sacramental service and pastoral care.

The version of "online church" isn't the future, it's now . . . today. In fact, we're already behind the curve because it's where the next two generations now live their lives. Our digital ministry work can no longer be an add-on to the Sunday service, it must become a core function, with an ability to impact people seven days a week; twenty-four hours per day.

By the way, this new world isn't springing up—it's already sprung; and the church better figure that out, or it will die trying.

Pastoral Care in a Brave New (Digital) World

I simply call this digital ministry the "pastor coach." Life coaching has been popular in the business world for many years and is easily adaptable in the digital ministry space. Pastors who learn to move from teaching to facilitating, from counseling to listening, from heavy-handed accountability to championing will find success.

Successful pastor coaches will adjust to a spiritual alignment model as we go out to the (social media) highways and byways. We'll be required to be openhanded to different cultures and thought as our ministry clients are no longer constrained by geography or norms. I see this modeled by my friend the Jewish rabbi.

"We prize our scripture much more than you," this rabbi told me, "but we allow the Torah to travel with us in community, not be stuck back in some past mindset around which we all must camp together."

His point was that gathering around community, rather than beliefs, allows even an atheist to still be Jewish and welcome at synagogue or seder. In the digital space, a pastor coach will need a humble theology as we find generations quite open to different forms of spirituality. We must minister to people where they are, not where we want to take them. I have coached a Buddhist, a humanist, a witch, and an atheist, and do so without demanding they change their beliefs in order for me to offer the love of heaven and freedom of Jesus to them. Likewise, Jesus wasn't losing status by sitting with the Samaritan woman at the well or having lunch with a "traitor" tax collector, despite these actions being *huge* violations of his position. Interestingly, the biblical text doesn't show Jesus feeling compelled to demand either person change their beliefs, yet each was transformed through their discussion and the free offer of relationship.

Being a Paraclete, Rather Than a Director

Like Jesus, a pastor coach must reach for relationship to effectively minister in the digital faith space. The Bible speaks of the Spirit of God, being a "paraclete" or one who walks alongside another. This is the work of the pastor coach; to walk alongside ministry clients to wherever their journey takes them. This is difficult for pastors who've followed the biblical definition of a shepherd leading the sheep through thickets they don't want to traverse in order to get to the shepherd's determined destination.

I find my predetermination of a ministry client's destination often limits other well-being opportunities that could arise as it limits our relationship. The ministry client realizes I have an agenda and our work together loses flow. Pastoral care is instruction and teaching—even indoctrinating; coaching is a collaborative search for answers inside the ministry client that requires listening over leading.

When I let my predeterminations go, and I trust the spirit of heaven instilled in every human being, I have the privilege of sharing in a uniquely surprising journey with each ministry client.

As you let go of party line answers to problems, and walk alongside instead, you may discover your ministry clients find answers for themselves that ultimately line up with heavenly truths. The Bible says God's eyes "range to and fro" seeking open hearts. When we learn to trust again the bigness of God's good spirit to do the heart work over our great teaching, we find that spirit big enough to do its work.

This allows me to engage every ministry client with the pure love of Jesus, and finding no need to judge their actions. We abandon the idea of right or wrong, good or bad during our work and give space for the ministry client's inner spiritual voice to share without shame why past behaviors occurred.

I use basic questions to get the pastor coach/ministry client relationship growing:

Are you good? Do you deserve good things to happen in your life?

When you did this thing that caused pain in your past, did you do so because you are inherently bad? Or because you had no other tools for survival or to dull pain?

What does spirituality look like to you and where does your inspiration come from?

Has anyone made you feel you didn't live up to their expectations?

What do you feel is your purpose in life?

As I draw out this inner dialogue, I resist the need to judge if that dialogue is from heaven or not. The fruit of the conversation will be evident as we continue in relationship. It's not that all voices inside are good, but each is telling a story that is valuable in moving the ministry client towards better well-being. When a patient goes to the doctor, they don't curse the pain and tell the patient to stop having it. The pain is the helpful tool that allows the doctor to begin diagnosing the problem inside. It's no different with emotional health. Any revealed unhealthy inner dialogue provides opportunity for finding its genesis in order to recraft the client's self-story with a more empowering one. Isn't this what Jesus said he came to do? To set captives free? To *sozo* people—to restore them body, mind, and soul?

But, What about Sin?

We've been taught that sin means "missing the mark." That definition, however, requires a set target to determine marks hit and missed. In pastor coaching, I treat "sin" as human attempts to have their needs met in unhealthy ways that injure relationship with another person. In this model, sin is simply failing to "love your neighbor as yourself." The Bible's description of this is people not knowing "their right hand from their left."

My observation is that every human action is a response to one of three human needs: safety, value, and purpose. All of us consider murder to be wrong, yet most of us do not consider it sinful if done in self-defense. Why? Because our safety is a basic human need and if violence is the only tool we have available to secure it, we believe it's not a violation. Similarly, this standard can be applied to the human search for value or purpose.

One ministry client of mine carried great shame for a teenage sexual relationship, which happened at a time when this person was leading worship services each week in their church. The shame carried by this person was palpable even many years after the fact.

I asked "Did you engage in this relationship because you are inherently bad? Or did it seem to meet a need to feel valued?"

As the ministry client considered my question, their inner dialogue revealed the underlying issue of a Christian father who lacked the ability to express affection. This revelation removed the shame from the ministry client and gave a pathway to move forward with a new, healthier inner dialogue. I pronounced forgiveness for this person and they were able to forgive themselves. This person didn't need rules to avoid such behavior in the future, but now carried a strengthened self-value that wouldn't allow such an unhealthy relationship again.

As we release thin interpretations of theology and even the "Christian-eze" of our traditions and language, we make ourselves more accessible to those who might be triggered by an "opening prayer" and run from relationship. While I do often use the Bible as inspiration or for application, I rarely say things like "the Bible tells us . . ." Instead, I couch Scripture in language more easily apprehended like "there's a proverb that says . . ." or "a biblical story I find helpful tells us . . ." Never forget "sinners" flocked to see Jesus. If our claim to Jesus' name triggers people away from us, rather than drawing them to us, are we perhaps "missing the mark" in demanding clients meet us in our religious/spiritual space, rather than us adjusting to meet them in a space in which they feel safe? Isn't that what Jesus would do?

Relationship through a Computer Monitor?

True pastoral relationship doesn't require a cafe and a coffee cup nor a couch in a pastoral office. We must understand that for millennials and Gen Z, digital relationships *are* real relationship. These younger adults have grown up with a screen constantly in front of them, connecting through Xbox. They're not thrown by a lack of proximity in relationship.

A recent documentary told a story of this reality. Notre Dame football player Manti Te'o became famous not only for success on the field, but also for the tragic story of losing his fiancé to cancer in his senior season. There were interviews with Te'o and his family sharing their grief. One problem with the story: the fiancé didn't actually exist. Te'o found out he'd been "catfished," an online scam of a person pretending to be someone they're not—often posing as a different age and/or gender.

This story of fake relationship ironically demonstrates how deeply younger generations can build relationships online and through devices. If a man like Te'o can fall in love with someone he's never seen, how much more can we build relationship over Zoom through regular online conversations? I personally use an online therapist with an office hundreds of miles from me and I'm a business partner with two people whom I've never physically looked in the eye. Yet, each of these relationships is as intimate as if we lived next door.

Digital Ministry Logistics: Be Excellent

These days churches spend tens of thousands of dollars on high-end sound systems, video screens, and smoke machines to compete with the entertainment choices of our parishioners. While I did find sophistry in this, I always appreciated our desire for a polished presentation allowed by our reasonable budgets. To that end, may I suggest that a $19.99 microphone/camera hung on our computer monitor might not be our best presentation of our digital ministry office.

Spend money on good cameras, lighting, microphones, and even backdrops. Have the most powerful WiFi available. There's no reason to look bad, sound bad, or have technical glitches while trying to impact the lives of others.

Avoid getting overly cute with background effects. I prefer a clean office feel as opposed to the green screen picture of your last vacation. Wild posters, stuffed animals, and other knickknacks can be distracting. Some prefer the Zoom blur background, but have a light behind you to ensure the edges of your head and shoulders don't blur or completely disappear during a vulnerable moment in your work.

As for sound, I once used a $600 microphone with my computer. But no matter how good the sound that mic produced (and, trust me, a $600 mic sounds better than a $19.99 one) it was still being shoved into a small funnel of the internet. I sold my high-end mic and purchased three $99 ones and a $150 mixer/computer interface on Amazon that gives me excellent sound.

My biggest recommendation is a gadget called PlexiCam. I'm not doing an endorsement for this company but I haven't found anything like it. This plexiglass camera mount allows me to position my camera anywhere on my monitor horizontally or vertically. This corrects a problem that always bothered me in digital ministry of being forced to choose between watching my client's face on the screen or appear to be looking them in the eye.

With this plexiglass holder I can position the camera in front of my ministry client's face, so I can look directly at the camera and, thus, my ministry client, and still be able to watch their important facial expressions. This can be a powerful connection tool for holding the client's attention and demonstrating that I am listening to them.

I do tell my clients I may look away from them from time to time as I type notes during a pastoral coaching session. I do this to save transcription time. I assure the ministry client that I am only taking notes, not texting or checking my email (and it should go without saying we should not be sending texts or emails during a client session.)

I use an app called Evernote to secure my notes as I type them on a page I position directly beside my ministry clients face on the screen. This allows me to then share the info with my ministry client via email or chat and with my Salesforce data collection service. As much as possible I try to use my skill to type without looking at my fingers to be able to take notes without losing that eye contact with my client.

These are things I've learned in my time of pastoral coaching. We must never stop learning new technology and apps. No matter how much of an old dog we may feel we are, there are always new tricks in the online space to be learned. Subscribe to online marketing emails and follow trends on social media to stay current.

Online Curriculum: The 24/7 Coach

My online curriculum not only gives me an effective tool for working with ministry clients, but gives me greater reach as it's always available (and sellable) to a greater number of clients. The curriculum is able to be ever-evolving—we're no longer required to publish expensive, unchanging manuals.

My curriculum is a five module, twenty-one lesson program, the first lesson of which I offer for free as a loss leader. Each module has a theme that takes me on a journey with the ministry client:

- Identity

- Mindset

- Communication

- Vision

- Impact

There are four individual lessons in each module that I offer in audio and text (video to come soon.) Each lesson has an online journaling app at the end for ministry clients to share personal thoughts that are then sent to me. This helps facilitate the question asking I do in our one-on-one connections and I'm able to focus on areas of discussion and work that are significant to the client.

To deliver this curriculum, I use a platform called Podia, an excellent curriculum delivery platform and subscription service that easily takes payment and delivers what I need to ministry clients. The journaling program comes through a platform called Paperform. With the swift, never-ending movement of online platforms, I'm certain the companies I use will change often. Just realize the platforms are out there to help build what is needed in the digital ministry space.

Taking Time Away from the Screen

I've always loved the story in Mark 1 where the disciples are searching for Jesus. This story demonstrates the value Jesus placed on self-care. When working in the digital ministry space, we need to "go analog" every once in awhile. Make sure to walk, go to the gym, have good old coffee time with a friend, and hang out with family. Sabbatical is vital in any space, but maybe even more so in the often lonely space of online ministry from an empty home. Make sure your need for human connection isn't met only by ministry clients or Facebook interaction. Your well-being, and your ability to be powerful for others, depends on it.

The New Online Church: The Cohort

I was recently involved in an intensive therapy group where we sat in a circle and shared our life challenges with one another. Nobody held back. Many tears were shed. It was ugly, messy, raw—quite simply, it was the best church group ever.

While I love the one-on-one pastor coaching I do, the space I provide for community—or cohort learning—is equally powerful. I've found people willing to be paracletes to one another in an emotional and spiritual well-being journey vastly accelerates their healing process. When people become vulnerable together and root each other on in their vulnerability, they learn they're not unique and not alone in their need for better well-being.

I provide these "cohorts" as coaching spaces and sacred, sacramental space. In the coaching space we process curriculum topics together. In the sacred space, we share practical theological discussion and sacramental times, such as Communion or corporate mindfulness. Can this be "church" in the digital age? For those unable to go back to their church community, the online offering of the sacraments is life-giving. We allow anyone interested to partake in Communion. We even encourage people to grab whatever they have in their cabinet and not be overly worried about the appropriate juice and cracker.

It has been bothersome to colleagues that I do not even ask if those participating in Communion are Christian. In fact, we stream the event on TikTok, YouTube, and Facebook and encourage all to join in. Is that allowing people to "bring damnation and illness" onto themselves? I don't believe so. I see Communion as an invitation to interact with the body and sacrifice of Christ. Not an interaction to affirm our Christianity, but to confirm our connection to the spirit of heaven and to each other. I want everyone to feel welcome to take part. Remember, the breaking of bread often was a meal together. Therefore to me, the idea that one is doing something sinful by eating a cracker and drinking some juice is not worth withholding connection from lonely people. This is the beauty of the digital ministry harvest field.

We even do baptism through livestreaming. There's no law that says I have to be the one to dunk somebody under the water, but I can be available online to bless that moment. I provide the pastoral cover and endorse those in spiritual connection to baptize.

Other Stuff

Titles

Many have asked me if we call ourselves "pastor" in the digital ministry space. I call myself Pastor Paul as an online marketing tool and I'm also ordained. Sometimes I feel titles can be pretentious, but I'm aware of the need some have for a pastoral authority to give them permission to be on their journey, so I gladly walk as their "pastor" even as we figure it all out.

Christian Works

The never-ending command of the Bible is to take care of the poor, foreigner, marginalized, and widow. Without an in-person, big-box church meeting, there will no longer be backpack drives, homeless feeds, and mission trips to offer in order for people to "check that off" their Christian task list. This is a blessing.

Remind your ministry clients that the Bible tells us to spur one another towards love and good deeds. Therefore, they need to find spaces to give their finances, time, and assistance in order to follow the biblical mandate. When people do this work out of their heart, rather than with a church effort (earnest or not,) that work is much more likely to feel purposeful to the ministry client. Encourage your people to find a cause and rally with others interested in that cause. Have them gather a group around a topic such as systemic racism and learn in a way they never could in church. Teach them to work alongside those in historically disadvantaged communities, rather than parachuting in as the Christian saviors who then disappear at the end of the task.

Licensing and Accountability

There was no licensing denomination in the new movement of the New Testament, just people with a call of heaven on their lives gathering together and laying hands on the ones being sent out. We can do the same. Yes, in our culture we do need a 501c(3) to officially "marry and bury" but let's do so through relationship—and be accountable to one another in the same way, so as to avoid rebuilding religious systems that no longer fit in the digital faith space. My group has a foundation that licenses pastors and has a goal for funding pastors leaving the ministry (which is happening at record rates) to train and serve in the digital ministry realm.

Marketing on Social Media

Yes, you may need to record yourself dancing onto your phone in order to attract attention to your work. You'll need to learn what a meme is, what trends and hashtags are, and follow closely the latest platforms for reaching your audience. Or hire a younger person to do it for you. Don't hate social media, embrace it. There's never been a better tool for letting the world know you exist and to promote the gift you are to the world. I'm 50+ years old and have nearly 120,000 followers on TikTok. Others have many more. It may be uncomfortable, but Jesus never called followers to comfort themselves, but to reach out to the masses. The masses today are on social media.

Should We Get Paid?

My ministry is a for-profit business. I know that's uncomfortable for some, but I believe the church is abusive of their not-for-profit tax status. The covenant of the 501c(3) between the church and culture was that the churches would do the community work of caring for the poor, marginalized, foreigner, and widow, and thus would return the value lost in taxes back to the community. Today, however, most churches spend 80 percent or more of their revenue on staff salaries, building cost and maintenance, and internal ministry. Add in the loss of property tax of the huge swaths of land used by our churches and, often, churches have become a net negative to the community. These churches often abuse their tax status while openly violating the law by promoting a political party and ideology.

Many of us are uncomfortable with the idea of getting paid for our ministry work. And I often encounter people who believe all pastors should give away their time and services for free. "Jesus didn't get paid" they say. Yet, we hear that Mary Magdalene, Joanna, and Susanna "provided for them (Jesus and his disciples) out of their resources." We don't know exactly how much financing these women provided, but we do know that through their support and the generosity of people who housed Jesus and his entourage as they travelled, there was enough money in the money purse for Judas to steal from it without being noticed by others. Does this mean we should be rich? I'll leave that up to you, but with openhanded generosity, I encourage pastor coaches to know the value of your time and that there's an audience willing to pay for the gifts you bring. Charge a fee, provide curriculum, or just give a Venmo QR code and ask people to give out of their ability and heart. I've found, by the way, that people who pay directly for a service value that service much more than those given access for free. Ultimately, I've seen more lives impacted in three years of online coaching than in twenty-five years of leadership and as senior pastor of a church.

Why Do Digital Ministry?

Listen to this comment I received from a former client just this week:

> *I have lost almost 30 pounds since we have ended our little group meetings. I cannot thank you enough for the encouragement that you've been to me to make myself matter to me. 33 more to go! I have even made an appointment to see a doctor for the first time in like four years. Because I am learning to love myself!*

When I responded to the client that it wasn't me that had done this, but they that had accomplished this because of the greatness inside of them, they responded:

> *No! You simply don't realize you have been a lifesaver to me.*

If a person can't understand the value of the gifts we provide, that's OK, they have the old churches available to help. I do give away a portion of my work time each week to people I feel deserve the care even though they have no means to pay. I must be a good steward of the resources I have, and time is the most limited of all. And, truly, many who say they can't pay, actually can, they've just been trained to think they should receive care for free or are unwilling to prioritize their well-being, which means chances of success in their work will be limited. Almost universally I've had more success with those who pay for my walking alongside than those who've been given my time for free.

Last thing, if a person is only willing to give when they get a tax break from the IRS for it, remind them that they get to choose if their financial reward for supporting a spiritual leader can come from Washington, DC before next April 15, or an eternal reward in heaven.

Pastor coach, *don't be afraid to ask for remuneration for your work*. You should expect to have enough money to live so that you can minister powerfully as a person whose basic needs are taken into account.

Conclusion

Yeah, the church realm better perceive this new digital ministry space as church attendance is shrinking. Jesus said of the religious system in his day "not one stone of that thing will stand on another" and did not beseech his disciples to pray that God would relent. I believe the voice of heaven is saying similar things today. But while this idea might cause us to lament, as the Old Testament prophets did, it's also a hopeful one. Something new is springing up, are you able to perceive it?

Pastor Paul Swearengin (he/him) is known for asking questions of the church and of culture that others may not feel free to express. He has a passion for truth and a heart for people to be freed from shame and condemnation in order to know their true value and purpose. After being trained and ordained for ministry by the Vineyard Association of Churches, Paul founded and led an evangelical church in Fresno, California for more than ten years. He chose to leave his position of leadership to become a creator, author, podcaster, and spiritual well-being coach. As "Unconventional Pastor Paul" on social media, Paul inspires and supports those who are questioning their faith and political views in an era of spiritual and social upheaval. Paul served as a longtime popular TV and radio sportscaster and radio business owner in central California. Inspired by their faith, Paul and his wife Ashley left their careers in order to "seek the welfare of their city." Paul transitioned to full-time ministry while Ashley served as a two-term mayor of the city of Fresno (2008–2016). Each a graduate of California State University, Fresno, Paul and Ashley continue to enjoy their unconventional lives along with their two children, Sydney and Sam.

6

Rethinking Staffing and Leadership

Sammy Kelly

If you've ever discussed digital ministry with a group of people, you know there can be a wide array of opinions presented. In more professional settings, such as instructional courses and presentations, these positions may be articulated with respect and collegiality. Within public forums, like TikTok, you may be surprised how quickly you are labeled a heretic for promoting such an audacious concept. Of course, these comments can fly just as quickly from even the most respectable of colleagues.

You've heard it before. "Church is meant to be in-person." "You can't build relationships online." "Digital ministry isn't real ministry." There is no sense of wonder about what is possible. Instead, the opposer takes a stance of defiance, silencing any consideration of the benefits in play.

Unbeknownst to these internet trolls, most digital-minded ministry folks would agree that in-person connection is a significant part of ministry itself.

Of course, it is! We are embodied people who need to see, touch, and sense other human beings around us. We know embodiment was important to God who *chose* to embrace the fullness of humanity through Jesus Christ. There is no doubt that spending time in-person with others is necessary for our personal well-being. However, this necessity does not negate the world of opportunity in digital spaces.

This is why one of our favorite phrases at Digivangelism, the digital ministry company I founded with Michele Barra, is that "digital ministry *is* ministry."

Digital ministry is not meant to be an add-on sprinkled on top of your pastoral duties. Digital ministry is not another way to describe the "marketing" of your ministry activities. Digital ministry can be experienced among and within all of what previously has come to mind as ministry. It opens wide the door to a new space entirely with added opportunities for connection and ever changing rules from which to operate off of.

How monumental. How hopeful. How terrifying.

And how exactly does this look lived out in the life of the church? Or the life of the church staff, leadership, and volunteers for that matter?

As with any facet of church ministry, there is no exact science that will offer a one-size-fits-all solution for every faith community. There is no formula for optimal well-being of your staff or standard list of duties that can be followed to achieve digital ministry excellence. However, at this point, there has been enough trial and error for some best practices to emerge.

Digivangelism's mission is to help progressive leaders of spiritual communities share hope, healing, and light online. Our primary work over the past year has been developing free resources for these leaders to better understand the digital possibilities within their work. Besides my work with "Digi," as we nicknamed the company, I have served as youth director of a local parish, director of youth, young adult, and faith formation ministry within the Northeastern Pennsylvania Synod, and am a graduate of United Lutheran Seminary. Each of these opportunities have allowed me to better understand the life of the church and the ways a digital experience weaves into the work we're already doing.

One of the most important lessons I have learned from my many digital functions is that to get comfortable on a new platform or with a new program, you first have to get used to being uncomfortable. Not necessarily in an unsafe or concerning way, but rather the discomfort that is felt when you lose a bit of control. When you acquaint yourself with a new function online, you do not yet fully understand how to operate the system. You must rely on the people around you to carry you along until you orient yourself. It's unpleasant and potentially overwhelming.

If you experienced this feeling while trying a new digital process during the pandemic, you know what I'm talking about. But this isn't an isolated experience that you overcome and leave in the past. This is the constant ebb and flow of using the internet for ministry. Technology advances. It will continue to advance. We must learn to find peace within the inevitable discomfort of learning with the growing digital landscape before us.

Maintain Focus on a Common Vision

It is one thing to learn to adapt your communication practices to an ever-changing digital environment. It is quite another thing to lead a team through these continuous adaptations, especially when none of you were trained for this work.

Some of these adaptations are required of us as technology inevitably advances. Just a few years ago, the conversations about what platforms to focus on sounded very different than it does today. TikTok came onto the scene and changed everything; it won't be the last platform to do so.

Other adaptations are required when implementing a more remote work environment for staff. Removing a required work location from the staffing arrangement presents a sense of distance into the leadership team. This physical distance can cause a staff unit to feel emotionally distanced if not tended to carefully.

The adaptations do not stop there as a remote staff may grow to realize they are able to work toward a common goal not only in different spaces, but at varied times, within multiple time zones, with separate groups of people, and even on unique projects. Suddenly, this separation of physical space means all the difference!

This makes the group's common mission or goal even more important. Start there.

Before your staff ever agrees to separate by space or time, make sure you are centrally focused on a shared vision. On a macro scale, it is likely the mission of your faith community that drives you forward together. On a micro level, you may have specific focuses for various weeks and seasons of the year ahead.

One practice Michele and I have implemented in our digital ministry work is to start every meeting with a sense of "drama," as described in the book *Death By Meeting* by Patrick Lencioni. The idea is to constantly center ourselves on the conflict that our mission addresses. This is not a meaningless practice of repetition, but an intentional refocusing on our purpose.

What problem does Digi address? Well, some of the most inclusive, loving, and devoted faith leaders are out there right now completely missing the people they want to reach with a message of love and light. It is our responsibility to help them significantly improve the lives of the people who need their message the most.

What about *your* community? What are your leaders centered on? Can you consider your mission in the sense of solving a conflict that is present in the lives of your people or community?

It truly has been centering to maintain this practice within each of our meetings. In ministry, there may be dozens of tasks any one person focuses on at a time. This number multiplies in the coordination of leaders working together. It's easy to be moving a million miles an hour in several directions. Centering on your purpose as a team is not only important, it is essential.

While the methods of centering a team outlined in *Death By Meeting* have worked for Michele and me, they are not the only ways to align your people and ensure everyone is laser focused on a common vision. You can likely dream up more creative ways that are more appropriate for your specific team and community.

The point is to continuously rally your staff and leaders around a shared goal. This must be prioritized to constantly remain conscious of and connected to your "*why*" as a team. Especially when your team is not only working on different projects, but in completely different spaces and times from one another.

Maintaining a Connected Team

There are many ways to experience connection with other people. These opportunities are gifts to humanity. The Creator formed us in a way which allows us to experience physical and emotional sensations when interacting with others. A warm embrace can bring us unmatched comfort. A thoughtful message can deeply impact us with joy. A rousing discourse with a colleague can stimulate our mind for days.

People need other people. We are wired for connection, driven by it, and our lives are enhanced because of it. Which is why there needs to be an intentional focus on maintaining a connected team through our ministry work.

However, this team connection must be based on more than work efforts alone. Relationships are built on more than striving toward a common vision. Relationships are built in the pauses in between breaths, the wardrobe compliments, the shared stories of another night with a new puppy, sick child, or snowy driveway to shovel. How do you build an authentic bond while remaining efficient in a digital working environment?

One of the first things to consider when determining how to keep your team connected is what type of working hours your team will operate on. There are numerous possibilities for a physically distanced staff dynamic.

For example, some leaders require all staff to be working and available within the same set hours. This environment mimics that of an in-person working arrangement. The team may not all be in one location, but they are all available and communicating throughout a designated working time frame.

Other communities allow staff to work whatever hours they prefer. Appropriate supervisory meetings and working meetings may be required on occasion, but for the most part, leaders are able to work on their own time and reach out as needed. While potentially unconventional, this arrangement often brings a new level of value to their lives—allowing them to work around their preferred sleeping schedule, family activities, appointments, and life responsibilities.

Some communities meet somewhere in the middle of these options, requiring standing meeting times or overlapping hours of availability, but not expecting anywhere close to a traditional full-time workday. This allows leadership to count on regular opportunities for connection with other staff, without expecting the constant daytime availability consistent with more standard in-office work hours.

It is important to make the expectations of your staff's availability clear to everyone. It is far better to overcommunicate the expected dynamic than to keep people guessing. Insufficient clarity fosters an environment where some leaders may become resentful that other leaders are not following the protocols they assume apply.

Regardless of the level of face time you have with staff, you need to be proactive about fostering relationships with the team. This could look like planned in-person outings, digital devotional sessions, or fun-focused synchronous or asynchronous conversations where leaders are encouraged to shift their focus from work to one another.

Some teams may have success incorporating time for general discussion and sharing at the start of regular meetings. Others may find this unproductive and prefer a scheduled or asynchronous time or space devoted purely to non-job related functions.

This intentional time of relationship building may be trickier now than at the start of the pandemic. While many of us are more equipped than ever with tools and experience of how to foster our relationships online, these digital possibilities have lost the sparkle they once had at the start of our time in quarantine.

A way to combat this could be to start an asynchronous thread where you can reflect on something non-work related once per week. Perhaps it could be a funny moment or moment of gratitude from your week every week in a Discord channel—or Marco Polo chat, or Mighty Network thread, if that works best for your people. It could be a commitment to share one photo per week of life outside of work. Perhaps it is a monthly check-in where you review the things you are looking forward to in the coming month. The purpose of this practice is to connect with one another beyond your ministry functions. Build some rapport for the people you are on a shared mission with, even if you don't see them every day.

Another practice to incorporate into your leadership is to celebrate birthdays, milestones, and work anniversaries well. If your team embraces a remote dynamic, you may have limited, if any, in-person time together, but there are always ways you can go the extra mile to make sure every member of your leadership knows they are valued, seen, and heard.

Knowing Your Tools

Now that you've solidified your focus as a leadership in one centralized direction and understand clearly how your team will digitally connect, it is time to decide what tools will serve you best in living out this mission online.

Unfortunately, you likely will not be able to utilize as many platforms and software as you'd like. This goes beyond social media. Not only is it impossible to be active on every communication channel possible, it's also wildly impractical to take on more than a handful at one time. Imagine trying to monitor email inquiries, Facebook messages and comments, new Google Form submissions, phone calls and text messages, Instagram DMs, YouTube comments, and TikTok trolls all at once . . . maybe you don't have to imagine.

Intentionally choosing the tools to communicate with your community may mean you need to make difficult decisions. To focus well on any one thing typically means holding strong limits against any competing options. This does not mean that you need to limit yourself to what you've known and used for the past decade, but it does mean limiting the directions in which you move forward. Especially as you embrace digital ministry anew.

Let's take a closer look at some tools which have been successful for ministry leaders.

Email

It's likely that you will use email for communication in some way, shape, or form. Most people are used to responding to email as part of their work responsibilities. However, it can be helpful to have some conversation about how quickly everyone is expected to reply to work emails. Without some guidance, leaders will create their own assumptions from whatever previous experience they bring into your community.

Slack

While many corporate offices make use of the free software Slack, it is not discussed as frequently in ministry contexts. However, with its ability to organize communication into various channels based on the topic or people involved, it is worth your consideration. Slack operates as an instant messaging platform, typically set up with multiple channels to keep conversations separated and on topic. There are dozens of add-on features for Slack, from incorporating GIFs into your messages to connecting your Google Calendar for automatic updates to an easy Zoom meeting command prompt that initiates a video conference on the spot.

With increased possibilities for digital connection comes an increased need for communication of expectations surrounding this tool. As we asked in the email section, how quickly are staff expected to respond to Slack messages? This may be a different answer than email. Speaking of email, what types of conversations should take place via email vs. Slack? How do these conversations differ from those that take place via phone calls, text messages, or in-person, if applicable?

Your answer to all of these questions will depend greatly on what level of accessibility you expect from staff, as indicated earlier. If your leadership is allowed to work whenever they want as long as their hours and work responsibilities are accomplished, you may need to wait a few days for email or Slack responses. If your team is expected to be online and available from 9 AM until 5 PM each weekday, a reply may be expected within a matter of minutes. Typically, Slack is a quick communication option as opposed to email, but this can be completely community dependent. If you decide to utilize Slack simply for its organizational capabilities, you may be okay with leaders checking it as frequently or less frequently than they check their email.

Cell Phone

We can't forget about tried-and-true phone calls, in addition to text messages, Facetime calls, and social media apps. Phone calls may be a more practical way to reach someone quickly, as long as it is clear ahead of time how available leaders need to be via their cell phones.

Text messages, Facetime calls, and social media apps may be less ideal for frequent professional discourse, but may be the best option from time to time. Because we often use these digital channels for more personal conversations than we may use Slack or email, it can be tricky to balance using our phones for more official use.

Free Google Apps

I truly do not know how I would function without the suite of free Google platforms available to anyone with a free Gmail (Google email) account. If you are unfamiliar with these, they mimic popular Microsoft features such as Word, Excel, and PowerPoint. These free applications allow real-time editing of documents, spreadsheets, presentations, forms, and more, at the same time, by multiple people. This means you and a team can build a policy doc, poll form, or worship presentation simultaneously.

There is also a fantastic URL shortcut for each of these platforms which I use just about daily. Typing "docs.new" into the address bar will start a new Google Doc under whatever Gmail account you are currently logged into. "Sheets.new" will start a new spreadsheet, "forms.new" begins a new poll," and so on and so forth.

Zoom

At this point many of us have been on at least one, if not one thousand, Zoom meetings. However, it's worth mentioning that Zoom meetings still certainly have a helpful function in any sort of distanced collaborative ministry. As always, be intentional about what type of accessibility you expect of your people. Pay attention to how many regular Zoom meetings they are part of and whether all are necessary. If all are necessary, do they all need to be as long as they currently run? It's easy to settle into a meeting and not realize how many minutes are slowly ticking away. Respect your team's time and attention; keep your meetings as efficient as possible.

Microsoft Teams

Teams is often compared with Zoom and Skype. It serves a similar function as both of these platforms and is a worthy competitor for either, with related features and integrations. While I have less experience with this platform personally, I know others who are happy using it.

Trello (Or Any Project Management Software)

With Google Drives filling up with Google Docs, Sheets, and more and more Slack channel conversations moving quickly, it is easy to find yourself in a digital disorganized mess. Project management tools help organize files and projects, allowing you to share your organization with others who can add to the mix. This can help keep everyone on task and organized.

While most of my personal and professional work has been with Trello, there are many project management tools out there for digital use. One benefit of Trello is that most of the useful features can be utilized on a free account. This may make it even more enticing for ministry use!

Moving Forward Technologically

You can deeply explore each of these options and read all of the reviews, but at some point you will need to decide how you and your team will move forward. My recommendation would be to make a decision and stick with it. There will be pros and cons to any situation, but it's far better that your team learns to work with whatever system you decide on than to make them constantly relearn new ones. If you need to update the terms of how accessible people will be along the way, do so. But do not require them to learn four different project management tools before you make a final decision.

Speaking of learning new tools, be sure to provide as much information for how to use the tools as possible. Many of these platforms already have how-to videos available for sharing. Make use of them! It may also be helpful to create some of your own instructions for how your leaders specifically make use of various platforms. What is appropriate to post in each Slack channel? Are emojis and GIFs welcome? Are they encouraged? How should you contact leadership for a nonurgent matter vs. an urgent one? Are there options in between?

With all of these avenues for connection, at some point, technology can become distracting to the actual functions of our work. Make sure not to expect staff to monitor too many platforms too frequently. Expecting someone to reply to every phone call or text, email, Slack notification, and Trello update within a matter of minutes is a surefire way to make sure they never have room for the necessary deep focus that is part of any creative endeavor.

Sharing Responsibility

Most faith leaders I have worked with are not opposed to sharing leadership. In fact, they long to fill their ministry with folks who are particularly called to the specific role they fill. The struggle is to find people who are willing to fill these necessary roles in the first place—not to mention the list of ideal roles that could be developed with additional digital ministry opportunities.

A helpful practice to make volunteer roles more approachable is to define the need as clearly as possible. People often do not want to commit to something they cannot understand. They may wonder, "Who will train me for this role? How much time is expected of me? What happens if I don't enjoy it? Who would I go to with questions?" Consider how many of these questions you are able to answer ahead of time.

Think about how flexible your community is able to be with volunteer schedules as well. It's no secret that people are busier than ever. Can the open role, potentially once shared by a long-time volunteer, be split into one that is shared by a rotating group of three or six? This changes a weekly volunteer role from a recurring commitment to an occasional opportunity to serve.

Faith leaders have witnessed this team approach work effectively with in-person cleaning teams, devotional leaders, youth groups, and musicians. It works just as well with shared digital roles. Instead of rotating who tends to the community garden, perhaps you rotate who asks the weekly thought-provoking question in the community forum. Instead of it being your month to think of icebreakers for youth group, perhaps it is your month to contemplate and film a few TikTok videos for the church account.

When it comes to finding the proper help for your digital ministry leadership, make sure to think outside the box. As you likely know well, you cannot ask the same people to do everything without overwhelming them. What other community participants or friends of the community could you include in your digital ministry efforts?

If your digital needs outnumber your options for assistance, think beyond the way you've "always done things." Is it finally time to hire someone to take on this role? If hiring a communications director (we'll talk more about that later) is not financially practical for your community, could an intern, contractor, or agency take on some of those duties at a more affordable rate?

If none of these options are feasible, consider where you may need to shift focus within your leadership. Are there areas of ministry that staff members are giving time to that can be replaced with a digital focus? This may look like a staff member finding a volunteer to help with one of the nights of in-person confirmation so that they can invest more time connecting with youth digitally. This might look like a leader finding their replacement for a particular ministry or event so they can focus on filming regular short form videos of themselves and others.

As you consider what is possible, focus closely on the gifts of the leaders involved. Technical skills can be taught as long as there is a willingness to learn, but unique talents and personality traits should be lifted up intentionally. For example, if you have someone in your community who is always asking thought-provoking questions, recognize this as a strength that can be exercised digitally. They could add live commentary and questions into the feed of any streamed sermon video. They could ask a weekly question in your community Facebook group, Discord workspace, or in a TikTok video. They could even help you think of additional questions for a pre-sermon or post-sermon online community conversation each week.

Sharing tasks with other volunteers, staff, contractors, and agencies can be overwhelming at first. They may be eager to assist, but you still need to be able to articulate your needs, expectations, and limitations. Make a list of all of the responsibilities you currently manage but need to off-load. Include ideal additions to this list. If you feel any sense of guilt in outsourcing these functions, remember that *no one* can do all things well. You sharing these duties with others is going to free you up to take a higher perspective, managing the work rather than completing it all yourself.

As you fill these roles, make sure there is a continual refocus on your community mission and goals. Those who come into your team from the outside may bring in their own processes and systems, but you will need to keep them centered on your community's purpose.

Digital Minister, Communications Director, Oh My!

There is no "right answer" for what a communications director does.

As with any ministry role, this can look very different for every community. And it should! The needs and makeup of every community will be unique. A cookie-cutter position cannot possibly work for everyone.

There are an infinite number of possibilities for how a communications director or digital minister can spend their time. The trick is to find the most impactful and valuable responsibilities for each community. When hiring someone for this role, it can be helpful to have some idea of what you expect of them. If you are less knowledgeable about digital ministry, it would be wise to leave room for flexibility in this position, intentionally seeking someone who can assist in your online ministry strategy.

As the digital mouthpiece of your community, it is important that this person becomes quickly connected to your mission and leadership. There needs to be a close link between your pastor, ministry staff, and the person who oversees the digital experience of your community. Ideally, this person does more than create a few nice designs and post them on your social media accounts. This is someone who deeply understands how the community should be presented for new folks, how the community itself best experiences digital connection, and how to help various ministries, volunteers, and staff share their faithful work online.

How this is lived out may vary depending on the size of your team and community. This leader may not create all these digital opportunities and assets, but instead manage the systems and people who do. Alternatively, they may be the one who does it all, gathering inspiration and content from other leaders and distributing it online.

This leader, and any online-focused leaders, must also be on the lookout for digital information to distribute to leadership who may be less in touch with online ministry offerings. They should keep an eye out for digital trends, how the community can participate in trends, analytics, and responses to current digital content. This information can be shared with other leadership to collectively decide how the community should best move forward in response.

New Priorities of Self-Care

New plans for operating online come with a renewed need for self-care. While many people gained experience in remote work during the pandemic, everyone's experience was unique. We have also learned quite a few things about taking care of ourselves since then.

Here are my best digital self-care tips for you and your leadership:

Encourage In-Person Community

As long as it is safe for your leaders to do so, encourage them to regularly spend time in-person with other human beings. This may look different for every member of your leadership, but all expressions should be valued. Dinner with friends? Lovely. Exercising at a local gym? Fantastic. Participating in a faith community offering? Perfect. Signing up for a class or membership? Whatever it takes!

Digital ministry is extremely important in this day and age, but you must pursue a personal balance. This may come naturally to your leadership, but some team members may need additional encouragement to prioritize this.

Incorporate Offline Time

Everyone needs time away from screens. And no, sleeping cannot be your only offline experience! Encourage your team's non-digital hobbies. One way Michele and I do this is by regularly checking in on each others' walks. A simple, "This weather is beautiful, are you able to schedule a walk today?" can be all the nudge that is needed to remind the other person to physically detach their eyeballs from the computer screen and take some time out of the office.

Maintain Flexibility and Understanding

If someone is struggling to stick to a designated timeline, start with curiosity rather than reprimands or passive-aggressive sarcasm. Deadlines are important and should be respected. However, there could be more going on behind the scenes. This can be especially difficult to gauge when everyone is working at different times from their own spaces.

If it becomes a chronic issue, consider building in regular check-ins to keep closer tabs on productivity. There should be accountability when targets are not met, but sometimes the difficulties are less about the work and more about the life situations the person is navigating.

Model and Support Deep Work

It would be nearly impossible to expect team members to get any sort of productive work done if you require them to reply to comments on every platform and communication channel within a matter of minutes. At some point, after constant interruptions of notifications and messages, our brains lose the ability to focus on one task for an extended period of time.

To combat these distractions, build in intentional times for deep work, where you maintain complete focus on the project at hand for a set amount of time. Model these sessions with your team, where you are unreachable and particularly engaged in a specific project. Support them in their own sessions, whether it looks like minutes/hours they are unreachable on Slack or an entire day each week they are gifted to focus on creative projects and planning rather than meetings and email responses. Giving leaders this space for focused efforts is sure to benefit their mental health as well as your ministry.

Digital Ministry *is* Ministry

Digital ministry can feel extremely overwhelming, but much of the basics are already built into your practice as a faith leader.

You already know how to focus on your mission and message, rethink and adapt your staffing situation, learn new tools and systems, love your leaders well over and over, remain attentive to self-care, encourage the gifts of others, and constantly reevaluate what is working.

The trick is to put it into action in an altogether new arena without letting the learning curve discourage you. The fundamentals are the same as they've always been. The way you live them out may look nothing like it ever has before for you, but as I mentioned earlier, technical skills can be taught as long as there is a willingness to learn.

Maintain this mindset as a student of the ever-changing digital world, fill your team with faithful leaders who have unique strengths from your own, and hold tight to your calling to love people in the way only you can.

The impact you make through your community's digital presence is an immeasurable gift bringing hope, healing, and light to those who may never experience it any other way. In the times when this work is more frustrating and confusing than you ever anticipated, may that simple fact be enough to keep you going.

Sammy Kelly (she/her) is the face of *Digivangelism,* a company dedicated to helping progressive leaders of spiritual communities share hope, healing, and light online. She is a graduate of United

Lutheran Seminary and has experience in youth, parish, and denominational ministry. She owns a video editing company and believes strongly in the power of video to connect with people and change lives. In her free time you can find her training in martial arts, running, scrolling through van builds, or petting the closest dog she can find.

7

Becoming a Digital Evangelist

Rev. Brandan Robertson

Progressive faith communities are rightfully skeptical of the language of "evangelism". In modern history, the word has come to mean something like "forceful conversion" rather than a demonstration of and an invitation to the way of Jesus. The communities that have defined themselves by their commitment to evangelism have, more often than not, been communities who are also committed to launching a political crusade to institutionalize their beliefs and values, forcing entire nations to align with and conform to their worldview. This so-called evangelism would more accurately be called "colonialism". However, progressives fear being identified with those who stand on street corners screaming at passerbys about their hell bound fate has prevented us from heeding one of the central commands of Jesus—publicly inviting others to his new way of seeing and being. Of course, most of us do not believe that joining the Christian religion or believing certain doctrines is a prerequisite to receive God's love or saving grace, but we *should* believe that the message we've devoted our lives to is worth sharing with others, right? By letting our fear of being identified with evangelicals drive our behavior, many mainline and progressive communities have forsaken any effort to actively invite others to consider the transformative message of the Gospel of Christ.

I am a millennial, which means I've grown up in a digital world. I don't remember a time before the internet or personal computers, and have lived most of my life with a smartphone in my pocket and some version of social media at my disposal. This also means that as a committed Christian, I've often utilized the internet to share aspects of my faith with my friends and followers across the internet. Whether through blogging, making YouTube videos, hosting internet radio shows, podcasting, making memes, sharing on Facebook, or composing Tweets, I, like a vast majority of people of faith on the internet, have talked about my faith and in so doing, invited others to consider the Christian faith path. Since the age of twelve when I began doing this, I've interacted with millions of people on the internet, engaging in robust conversations and debates, sharing deeply personal stories, and forming profound bonds around our shared faith journeys. As my faith has evolved, much of this content creation online has focused on helping people separate Jesus from the institutions that bear his name and discover a progressive, inclusive way of being a Christian. This was just a natural part of my engagement online—my faith was important to me, so I posted about it, and often was given incredible opportunities to invite others to this path. I never considered this "evangelism," though I'd argue it was.

In the internet age, where our whole lives are lived as hybrid existences between the digital world and the "real world", a growing number of us are sharing more of ourselves more vulnerably on social media which is creating profound connections with strangers and giving us opportunities to share "the hope within us" (1 Peter 3:15), even as we offer critiques of corrupt political actions, retweet inspirational quotes, or post photos about beautiful moments of our lives. This is precisely what it means to "evangelize"—to embody good news to the world around us.

Everyone is an Influencer

In this digital age, every person is an evangelist (or in modern vernacular, an "influencer"). Every person has the ability to reach hundreds of thousands of people every time they engage on social media. The question we must ask ourselves is *what are we evangelists for?* A simple scroll through our feeds on any of our social networks will quickly reveal this answer—is it our political party? Fitness? Sports? Parenting? What kind of content are we posting and regularly interacting with? And is it in alignment with the faith we claim as our foundation and core identity?

What I am not suggesting is that everyone should devote their social media to religious content from here on out—especially if that would be inauthentic to how you embody your faith. Rather, I am suggesting that progressive followers of Christ be mindful of the messages we are sharing and how we might inject a bit of hope into the cynical world we now live in, and how we might express our faith-rooted values as we engage in social media. This is something "evangelicals" have done very well for a long time— evangelical communities have been effectively using digital media since the early 2000s, livestreaming their services, creating robust social media content, and encouraging their communities to like, share, and create their own faith-rooted content. But the playing field has at last been leveled after the COVID-19 pandemic—virtually every person and community in the world is now connected to social media and has equal access to the billions of people who are on the internet around the world. Why would we not use this moment to articulate a progressive, inclusive faith that challenges the corrupt and diluted versions of Christianity that have been promulgated so loudly for so long?

My TikTok Transformation

My passion around using social media for evangelism really emerged at the beginning of the COVID-19 pandemic in 2020 when I decided to download TikTok. With our church closed down, I found myself with some extra time on my hands and I had seem a number of my clergy friends posting fun little TikTok videos on Facebook and Instagram of them dancing in their collars or declaring God's love for all with some trending song in the background. I figured I would jump on to see what all the hype was about. After I posted a few cringe-worthy videos of me dancing in my collar, I decided to begin an experiment where I would create thirty-second videos where I would talk about progressive Christian theology—my true passion. My first video was a flyby summary of why the Bible *didn't* condemn LGBTQ+ people. Then I did one on why hell didn't exist. I continued to make videos like this, and to my surprise, they began to rack up a *ton* of views—some of those early videos spiking to twenty thousand views within a day or two, and my follower count began to grow rapidly—five thousand, ten thousand, fifty thousand, and so on in the first few months. Then the comments and messages began flowing in— young people saying things like "If I had a pastor like you growing up, I'd still be a Christian" and "You're making me want to join the church again". Again, I didn't set out to convince people to become progressive Christians or join a church—but what became clear to me is that progressive, inclusive Christians have been really bad at letting others know we exist. My TikTok account became a gateway for hundreds of thousands of people to simply learn that there was another way to be a Christian—and many of those people had been yearning for such a way to be illuminated for them.

As my account continued to grow towards two hundred thousand followers and the comments streamed in by the thousands each day, it became clear to me that I needed to create a place where all of these individuals who were discovering progressive Christianity for the first time on TikTok could come together and have more substantial conversations. One way I began to do this was to utilize TikTok's "Live" feature (which is available to all accounts that have more than a thousand followers) which allowed me to go live and chat with my followers in real time, answering their questions and giving advice and guidance. Once a week, I would log on to TikTok and go live for about an hour—over the course of that hour,

1,500 people on average would listen in to my real-time conversation about theology and spirituality with those who had submitted questions.

After seeing this response, I began to promote a weekly Zoom gathering for my followers where we could see each other face-to-face and do a Bible study from a progressive perspective. Within a week of advertising this study, 750 people had registered, and on our first study, about two hundred people showed up to participate. There were people from remote parts of the world who didn't have a progressive church in their country who were so elated to be a part of a digital community, and young queer Christians whose families didn't support them that were discovering that there were in fact Christians who loved them just as they were. Night after night, once the study concluded, I would sit in silence, often tearing up at the blessing of being able to share my understanding of the Christian faith with these diverse people from around the world, and *actually* see it transforming their lives. After nearly four years of full-time parish ministry in a brick-and-mortar church, I, like many pastors, had begun to grow cynical about the faith and it's ability to have any tangible impact on people's lives or our world. Yet here, in the digital sanctuary created by this strange little social media app, I was getting to do *real* ministry that was healing *thousands* of people. I could have never imagined such an opportunity, nor did I ever think I would find a passion for "evangelism" again after leaving my conservative understanding of Christian faith. Yet here I was, a digital evangelist, being reminded that the good news of Jesus truly was "good news of great joy." (Luke 2:10)

Eventually, the impact of this digital evangelism helped me to step away from my brick-and-mortar church and devote myself to full-time digital ministry. I launched the *Metanoia Community*, which gathered folks from my TikTok on Zoom each week for Bible study, prayer, and meditation, and opened a Discord secure chat room for them to stay in conversation throughout the week. Nearly every week, I met one-on-one with folks from around the world who needed pastoral care and guidance, and also spent a good deal of time helping folks find inclusive churches in their geographical area that they could connect to. The opportunity of digital ministry became a full-time job for me, and in many ways was more life-giving than any ministry I had ever engaged in before because of the ability to have direct contact with and immediate impact on hundreds or thousands of people in real time.

On the Haters

I would be remiss to not mention the other side of the equation—while digital evangelism allows you to connect with those who have been yearning to hear an inclusive articulation of the Christian faith, it also will connect you to those who are staunch defenders of an exclusive understanding of the faith who will spend a lot of time commenting, messaging, and making video responses to your content that call you "false teacher," "heretic," and worse. As a gay Christian minister on TikTok, I've received threats of violence and have been the target of orchestrated campaigns to get my account banned or certain videos removed. It would be easy to say that I have always been able to "shrug it off," but these interactions do take a mental, spiritual, and emotional toll. In the same way that pastors of physical communities are encouraged to take regular breaks and find external support beyond their church communities, it has been vital that I have a regular rhythm of stepping back from TikTok for a week or two to regain my energy to engage in what can often be a combative environment. I've also become an avid user of the "block" feature, as well as utilizing TikTok's ability to ban certain words from being used in comments on my video. (I've added heretic, false teacher, demonic, repent etc. so that comments with those words no longer appear on my feed.) This is not only for my own well-being, but also for the well-being of those on my page who are beginning to rediscover the Christian faith, who can often be turned off upon seeing the hateful responses of other Christians on my videos suggesting that God's love extends to *everyone*, that being queer isn't a sin, or that Christian nationalism is antithetical to the message of Jesus.

An Unprecedented Opportunity

Since joining TikTok two years ago (at the time of this writing), I have witnessed dozens of other progressive Christian clergy and laypeople step into digital evangelism, collectively reaching millions of people with a version of the Christian faith that truly gives people hope. The impact of an individual clergy person or even lay person utilizing social media to share their faith cannot ever be accurately assessed, but what I can say for certain is that *everyone* who produces content online will reach, influence, and impact *someone*—whether you ever know it or not. In this emerging digital era, it is an act of negligence to ignore the opportunities we all have to share good news with a weary world through social media. The goal of course isn't to convert people to our religion, but to show people that there is a better way to orient our lives, a way that brings about a sense of purpose and that helps make the world a more just and beautiful place. This message—the true message of the gospel—is being drowned out by so many other messages that saturate social media spaces. We need as many people as possible to use their voice and perspective to create social media content that equips and inspires the seekers, cynical, and suspicious. It has never been easier to share our faith, to expand our digital sanctuaries, and to reach *millions* of people with hope and help for their lives.

If we do not seize upon this opportunity, we can be certain that the end of our churches is imminent. The future of the church is a hybrid of local community connecting to an international digital community, but in order to create such an extensive digital reach, we must be willing to step out into the digital dimension without fear, with creativity, and with commitment to showing up as our full selves, with our unique perspective, and trusting that God will use our voice to reach all whom it needs to reach. Whether you realize it or not, if you're on social media, you're a digital evangelist—the question, again, is for what? May we rise to the challenge and opportunity of this moment together.

Rev. Brandan Robertson (he/him) is a noted author, pastor, activist, and public theologian working at the intersections of spirituality, sexuality, and social renewal. A prolific writer, he is the author of nine books on spirituality, justice, and theology, including the INDIES Book of the Year Award Finalist *True Inclusion: Creating Communities of Radical Embrace.* In July 2021, *Rolling Stone* magazine included Robertson in its annual "Hot List" of top artists, creatives, and influencers who *"are giving us reason to be excited about the future."* Robertson received his Bachelor of Arts in Pastoral Ministry and Theology from Moody Bible Institute, his Master of Theological Studies from Iliff School of Theology, and his Master of Arts in Political Science and Public Administration from Eastern Illinois University. He is currently pursuing his PhD in Bible and Cultures from Drew University. He currently resides in New York City.

8

Meeting This Digital Moment with Faith

Rev. Dr. Floyd Thompkins

What is the lesson we can relearn from the twelve disciples of the Gospels and the early church of the New Testament in this fourth Industrial Revolution? What do we have in common in this digital age? Quite a lot.

The Christian faith was born from the actions of unlikely people. The twelve disciples of Scripture and most of the leading figures of the early church communities were unexpected leaders. Lydia, a business owner, a eunuch from Ethiopia, a fisherman from Capernaum, and their lot were people whose encounter with Jesus changed their lives and created a passion to change the lives of those around them. The people of "the Way" were innovators and risk takers. The churches were bold, courageous, and carried out a messy mission of empowerment and radical empathy. In Jesus' footsteps, the early church challenged the patterns the exploitation and exclusion in the religious culture around them—and their movement went viral.

Likewise, in our modern era, the digital space has given a voice to anyone and everyone to represent their faith and find (or create) their unique community. It also has given rise to different ways of calling people to worship or faith: a TikTok, a Facebook post, or a Tweet can be a whole sermon. Digital content creators have become new voices speaking to the masses and creating new communities and connections based on their faith. This process has democratized spiritual leadership and education. People have started to curate groups in their own unique and powerful ways across the internet.

Worship's byproduct is an empowered humanity that changes the world in the ways that Jesus changed the world, but, like many such movements of reform and innovation, if one is not thoughtful, the theological and structural evolution can stagnate as churches continue to perpetuate institutional structures that are more concerned with maintaining the status quo than with evolving towards the new thing the Spirit is leading us towards. For some, ministry has become merely a profession or credentialed activity. Power and confidence, sometimes by intention and sometimes accidentally, within the church leadership parallel the patterns of the patriarchy and empire. Those who are chosen to lead and those who feel they could lead devolve into the very patterns of exploitation and exclusion that Jesus and the early church challenged.

Patterns and Performance

The wide variety of worship practices within Christianity can be presumptuous and off-putting to people depending on their denominational background. I'm reminded of a colleague at San Francisco Theological Seminary who was startled when someone ended a prayer to open a meeting with the words "Lord in your mercy" and spontaneously everyone said, "Hear our prayer." It was a very Presbyterian practice, and she was not a Presbyterian. I grew up in the African American Southern Baptist tradition; growing up as an African American I always enjoyed and was fascinated by the reactions and observations from my non-brown friends who occasionally visited my church. We must admit that because our worshipping communities are embedded with rituals and assumptions unique to us, we sometimes lose the ability to see ourselves with the clarity of an outsider.

When I began "Black Church", a multicultural, ministerial effort at Stanford University, it was an intentional community striving for inclusion by defining *Black* as a rejected yet open community. Though we strove to embody openness and inclusion, eventually even this community became known by certain rituals or expected ways of worship and belief. It takes thoughtfulness and openness to continue to ask, "How do we worship together in ways that continue to widen our circle of inclusion?"

A lot of the time, Sunday Christian worship is performative. This is not to say that it is not sincere and authentic, but it is none the less performative. Sunday worship has an order. It has a time commitment. It has rote or expected lines. And, it has a soundtrack that enhances the effect of the whole performance. It is also effective but, like all good performances, unless you are a part of the production, one feels compelled to judge and react to the emotional effect of the moment. Leaders who may also practice faith have been given a professionalized model of worshipping: only ordained and approved people can lead worship and only these approved actors can authentically lead people in proper performance. Anyone could tell those who are cast members—adorned in church clothes and reacting to cues in worship indicating when they bow, raise their hands, dance, or stay quiet. All of this has led to the compartmentalizing of worship. It has also led to a cynicism about faith for many people. In our modern age, with every revelation that the cast of characters who lead the performance on Sundays are not in fact the character that they portrayed in their church, many people have begun to regard the church as fiction and have left feeling disillusioned. At the same time, new communities and leaders have stepped up outside of the traditional church space, creating well-produced worship spaces in the ever-expanding digital landscape, and fewer people found in-person Sunday worship worthy of their time and presence.

An Awakening Catalyzed by a Spike Protein

Even before the COVID-19 pandemic, there was something amiss with the worship. The script, images and, production did not seem to fit neither the message of the one to whom it was directed—Jesus of the Gospels—nor those to whom it was supposedly meant to benefit. Worship had become an operatic performance when it seemed that improvisational jazz was needed. Worship had taken on rules and dictated form, having the structure and function of an anchor, when it seemed that people needed wings to navigate and soar above the dizzying number of changes facing them in their lives. People needed a spiritual or religious language to help them live in the twenty-first century. In evangelical denominations, mainline denominations, and nondenominational churches, worship was losing the attention and attendance of an emerging generation that deemed it not relevant to their lives.

The COVID-19 pandemic forced the church to examine, for the first time in a long time, it's performance and evaluate it with clarity under the threat of possible extinction or necessary evolution. Church leaders had to ask: Why would someone dedicate time to a worship service? Do we need to have a worship service? What is worship? How shall we worship? In real time, the risk of ignoring these questions were greater than the possible pain of considering them. Scriptural platitudes and clutching to the traditions of past generations were ineffective talismans to ward off the questions of effective worship.

Curiously, worship is the most fluid act of faith. It is the most malleable to the diversity of human experiences. If it is to be revitalized it must become untethered from the idea of it being an organizing or defining character of a community. This assumption has led to the need to define a single or dominant expression of worship for a community. This is in total opposition to what worship looked like for early Christians who were enduring persecution and worshipping in homes and hovels, around dinner tables and in catacombs. Is there any doubt that each house or hovel had their own unique and powerful way to access the hope and promise of the divine?

Recognition of the Call

It is now an undeniable truth that a church or fellowship that is not "camera ready" or at least "media relevant" will not be effective or influential in the emerging digital era. After the COVID-19 pandemic, the ever-expanding number of livestreaming and digital community engagement options have created an abundance of possibilities that have overtaken the previous objections to using social media or digital avenues for worship. To be clear, this was already beginning to happen before the pandemic. Now, as the pandemic restrictions have lifted, a substantial number of those who previously attended in-person worship are choosing to stay home and demanding that the community find ways to help them participate digitally. These people combined with those who were already committed to digital consumption of their corporate worship have driven the necessity of questions about what it means to worship together. How is connection to be created and maintained in a mixed media environment?

TikTok, Facebook, Instagram, Patreon, and Twitter are all platforms created with the hope of connecting people and forming meaningful relationships online. They have become the native language of new generations and the learned language of older generations. The challenge is overcoming this tension and beginning to define what a successful leveraging of these platforms looks like; it still is mainly attendance and views, likes, and comments. This is not new. In previous generations, it was a count of people who physically attended church; now data analytics and a dashboard can provide the same information.

However, the novelty of the digital environment is that it is not one-way communication. There are outside algorithms assessing relevance and exposing churches to a wider and passionately opinionated communities. We are being forced to reconsider the two great questions of worship: How do we connect to God? How do we connect to one another? The church has, in lightning speed, been forced from its segregated isolation of religiously homogenous spaces to full exposure to the good, bad, and ugly of human community. Before this moment in history the church had literally been preaching to the choir—now, if the church is not relevant it will be relegated to a quaint anachronism.

The digital landscape is a bright light that demands clarity and passion because, if one does not do it for oneself, others will do it for you. This is good news for a community that is founded upon Jesus whose main purpose in Scripture is to define himself with absolute precision about who he is and why he is relevant. He was opinionated and passionate about the kind of community we should have. This robust proclamation is especially well suited for the digital environment. The safe institutionalized witness that the church had lapsed into is not a viable option. In truth, that "safe" witness had become unsafe for many whom Jesus had fought to include and enfranchised during his ministry.

We must shift to think of our digital attenders as an audience in order to think of the kind of content we will create, because logging off or clicking to another site is so easy one cannot assume patience or commitment. The visual and auditory experience have an enormous affect upon the weight of consideration from the audience. The digital environment requires that the worship service must be tailored for the limited space and respectful of the restraints time and attention span in a 2D environment.

A Warning

Because a Christian witness on the internet will often encounter the very same resistance, ridicule, and refutation that Jesus endured, the church can be tempted to succumb to the seduction of social media by simply absorbing or assimilating to the pervasive ethos of the medium by becoming argumentative and dismissive. The truth is that this kind of content reaps almost instant popularity, but results in a church fostering the conditions of tribalism and prejudice which is exactly the opposite of what Christ calls us to do. This model of digital witness abandons the aspirational ideal of connection between unlikely people with the purpose of building a better world for us all.

Everyone Is a Minister

The digital space is not primarily a place of teaching theology or religious polemics. Rather, digital witness is about testimony, life story, and consistent character. Online Christians are disciples and the way we conduct ourselves online is a way of worship. Jesus said to his original disciples "You are the light of the world," reminding them that their stories magnified the goodness, grace, and power of God. When people log on to a church's website or social media, they come as seekers. They seek information, community, support, and a place to be heard. Every user has a voice and therefore a unique witness. One's comments, likes, and presentations have immediate impact. In a 3D world the patterns of physical actions determine authenticity. In the virtual or 2D world, words and digital actions are the currency of legitimacy. One can craft any identity—everyone has total control of their message, image, and even with whom they choose to interact. Witness has never been more important and powerful as it is now, when we are connected to millions of people around the world in real time on the internet.

As with the original disciples, each person has their own presentation of the good news. The canonical gospels do not contain the whole story. They each are written for and to a specific community, and their context is the essential factor to understand accurately the content. Much of the misinterpretation or exploitation of the teachings of Scripture have arisen from subsequent generations' imposition of their community's reading back into the text their own values, for example the notions of slavery and women's role in churches, and every time, worship and witness have faltered under the rigidity of the church's historic march towards homogeneity and oppression. In our modern era, the church has yet again been caught flat-footed in the wake of the onslaught of historic, rapid, and unpredictable changes in the world. The history of defining creeds, setting our denominational boundaries, and creating a credentialed class of approved clerics has not served this present age well and they will not serve the new digital age either.

In the digital space, the work of creating an ethic and theology of worship has become an essential activity. There are literally millions of Johns, Matthews, Marks, and Lukes who will write and speak to their own communities in their own unique ways. They cannot be understood without the Rosetta Stone of their shared language, values, and concerns. The congregates of these communities are generally called "followers", and the collective voice of faith has never been louder.

As in the emerging days of the gospel of Jesus, not all these online communities are complimentary—some are indeed competitive. It is increasingly important the Christian leaders be supported by education and mentorship. The clerical roles are largely reserved for a particular community who will continue to meet in person. However, much of the light and power of the gospel is being led by those who are simply animated by faith, feel a sense of call, or simply possess the charisma to have influence online. Because of this shift in religious and spiritual leadership, new structures and approaches of theological and biblical education will have to be developed. Educational resources must be made affordable, accessible, and relatable. Stackable certificates will replace degrees. Curriculums will have to be responsive places to offer Christian wisdom, intellectual resources, and social tools to the new Christian digital leaders.

One Church or Two?

The biggest effect of the digital church, however, is the way in which its demands change the in-person worship. The question that must be considered carefully by each community is whether their digital church can coexist with their physical church. Are they parallel or intersecting? Are they two different expressions of church or are they in fact different churches?

The answer to these questions is driven by the in-person church community's ability to redefine community by its contemporary experience. With added mobility and new ways of communicating people's definition of friends and community have expanded in remarkable ways. People's lives have already been hybrid for some time. We all live in two worlds and have friends and loved ones that mean a great deal to us whom we may never meet in person but have a robust connection with online. In the future, this blurring of the non-digital and digital space will become more frequent, and as the Metaverse and virtual reality technology continue to emerge, they should not be ignored by the church. Church membership and church ministry must expand to incorporate worship that is relevant and moving for both environments simultaneously. It also must create a pastoral strategy that effectively supports the growth and spiritual health of all the people in the community—virtual and in-person.

There is no future in the church presenting an either-or answer to church membership and planning. People have already chosen. Investment in a new communication infrastructure and production equipment is an absolute must. Because this is a zero-sum equation in terms of resources, many churches will have the difficult conversations about continuing their current investments in their brick-and-mortar structures, or they will at least have to recognize that the function of its property should be repurposed and retrofitted to facilitate community and not have its space as the center of the community.

A Renewed Existence and Mission

In both the digital and in-person church the guiding principles of change are relevance and authenticity. Salvation continues to be the reason for the existence of the church. By this I do not mean the salvation of the church or the salvation of those in the church. But I mean genuine concern for the planet and all those who live upon it. Spirituality's impact upon the world has never been more needed. Spirituality is the language of connection, the sound of empathy, and the empowerment of humanity to build a future guided by God's imagination. The church, both in its in-person and digital form, must inspire a personal connection with the Divine and a deepening and more authentic transforming relationships with people. If it keeps its focus on helping people to find hope and meaning in the broken world, the church will always be relevant.

So the venue has changed, but the work remains the same. This is a time of disjointed communities, political and moral cynicism, and questioning of every social institution. The advances in communication have only serve to exacerbate a global existential anxiety—humanity is afraid that it lacks the capacity to survive this moment in time. The person and work of Jesus is needed to affirm a Divine presence that offers grace and mercy to all human beings with equal ability to change the world. The disciples and apostles of the New Testament, those original influencers, embraced the new possibilities for worship, the transformation of their faith, and empowered and enlarged their communities of belonging, doing much good in the world. Likewise, there is much to be gained as we strive to do like those earliest disciples, learning from the success and failures of our forebearers and peers as we carve out the places and encounters that our world so desperately needs in this emerging digital age.

Rev. Dr. Floyd Thompkins Jr. (he/him) is the current pastor of Saint Andrew Presbyterian Church in Marin City, California. He is the former Vice President of the Center for Innovation In Ministry at San Francisco Theological Seminary located in San Anselmo, California. Reverend Thompkins previously served as the assistant dean of the chapel of Princeton University and Associate Dean of the Chapel at Stanford University.

9

The Nuts and Bolts of a Digital Sanctuary

Stephen Hale

Much of this book has emphasized theological reflections on digital ministry. Of course, this is where we must begin. There are myriad questions that we must wrestle with. How appropriate is communion when we are not in the same physical space? How can we form community when we are not in the same physical space? However, embedded in these theological concerns are practical and logistical concerns. Whether or not true friendships can form on the internet is a theological question to some degree (everything is theological), but it is also a practical question. For another example, best practices in fostering conversation is a practical and logistical question.

When we combine our ministry goals with our theological and practical reflections, a strategy comes into focus. In my work with churches, the first question I ask is almost always "what are you trying to accomplish with your digital ministry, or your online worship?" Particularly during the pandemic, most churches I spoke with did not have much clarity about this question. This is understandable, of course. These are new questions for many of us!

On the other hand, many of these churches are embarking on expensive and resource-intensive programs without much of a plan.

My work with Capital Hope Media has enabled me to leverage my backgrounds in both pastoral ministry and audio/visual technology to help churches with their digital ministry. That is a somewhat unique position to be in, and it can help provide clarity as churches consider a ministry strategy. In this chapter, we will examine a few fundamental questions about ministry strategy, and compare them to the costs of livestreaming an in-person worship service. Once we see the costs in dollars and volunteers, some of us may determine our communities are simply unable to pay those costs. This is clarifying! Afterward, we will compare alternative ministry strategies which are markedly more affordable.

Three Different Audiences

As you begin to consider your church's approach to online ministry, consider roughly three different audiences you might engage with. Articulating what audiences you want to engage can clarify a great deal about what comes next.

To some, this question seems counterintuitive. Shouldn't your church be open to everyone? I think this question misunderstands a few things. The kingdom of God is for everyone, the gospel is for everyone, but your church is not. Any given (in-person) church is for a limited subset of people who happen to live in a certain geographic area, who happen to share some theological concerns, who happen to appreciate certain approaches to communication, who happen to enjoy certain kinds of music. Your worshipping community might welcome anyone who shows up. However, your worship service has been designed to meet the needs of certain persons, whether your church was conscious of that or not. When beginning a new ministry, it is wise to take stock of these questions. What audience, what group of people, do you primarily want to engage with this digital ministry?

The first audience is those who might be interested in your church from outside your church, but inside your local community. That is, your online ministry exists for people who do not currently attend your church, but might one day. This is related to the idea that a church's web presence is the new front door in our internet-saturated society. Almost no one will ever visit your church without looking at your website. Similarly, very few will ever visit without watching your video content. This first approach means connecting with your local community in an online space in a way that encourages them to attend your in-person worship. Notice, this perspective keeps the in-person service as primary, with digital ministry as something of an add-on.

The second audience is simply engaging members of your church who attend in-person services less often than they would like. You can consider soccer families here, who want to be in Sunday worship, but often have conflicts based on kids' activities. These families would often love a way to engage with Sunday morning worship on their own schedules. Perhaps they listen to the sermon on the Monday-morning drive to school, or Sunday evening when the family returns home. Also consider homebound folks who are unable to attend in-person worship as often as they might like. Digital community can create space for them to continue engaging with their church from home or even senior living communities.

The third audience is to create a distinct online community. You can think of this as a distinct worship service, or as a book study that meets online. Many examples of this audience have been discussed in this book, including Rev. Matt Hambrick's Accidental Saints group. Other examples could include livestreamed worship that essentially forms a community who exclusively attends the online worship.

Now, consider some typical approaches to digital ministry from the perspective of these three audiences. For a simple example, how well does a livestreamed version of Sunday morning worship meet the needs of these three different audiences? For those who are outside your church, a livestreamed worship service can represent your Sunday morning worship reasonably well. If this hypothetical person is already considering a visit to your in-person worship, livestreamed worship helps them understand what your in-person service is like. It also meets the needs of parishioners who are unable to be present on Sunday morning. That is, if you think of your Sunday morning in-person worship gathering as primary, with digital ministry as secondary, livestreaming that worship service is strategically appropriate.

However, livestreamed online worship is a trickier fit to create a distinct online community. It is possible, of course. People may gather online who love your pastor's sermons and worship music as much as those who gather in person. You could improve this with great hosts or digital pastors. On the other hand, if your goal is to create a distinct online community, there might be alternative approaches that are better suited to this goal.

Livestreamed worship is not the only approach to digital ministry. However, it does provide a helpful logistical landmark. For that reason, we will examine the costs of a true livestreamed worship service below. We do this for two further reasons. First, livestreamed worship is the most complex and expensive approach to digital ministry. It is also the approach many of us think of first when we think of digital ministry. For worshipping communities that have resources, livestreamed worship is low-hanging fruit. It doesn't take much imagination, and, truthfully, it can be done (poorly) without much of a plan. For these reasons, we will examine a baseline of the most affordable approach to livestreaming reasonably well. After examining the resources this approach requires, we will compare a few alternatives.

Some Assumptions

Before outlining one approach to reaching these audiences, we should clarify two assumptions. The first assumption is that we are trying to build community in an online space. That is, we are not simply creating digital content, we are fostering community. There will be more to say about doing this well when we discuss a ministry strategy.

The second assumption is that, however we communicate, we strive to do that well. We want to communicate well in any medium in which we operate. I am surprised how controversial this sometimes is. Consider, though, the pastor of your church. A good deal of her job is public speaking (i.e. preaching). Surely, she works to be a better communicator over time. While it would be unreasonable to expect most preachers to become one of the best preachers in the country, we still strive to communicate more and more effectively inside the medium of preaching. Consider the musicians in your church. I know of almost no churches that would long tolerate singers who could not sing (more or less) in tune. That is, we expect musicians to communicate somewhat well in their chosen medium of music. We may not expect perfection, or Hollywood-level talent (though some of our churches do), but we still expect some level of quality.

When it comes to video work, almost all readers instantly know what this means. Most of us grew up watching video on TV and in movie theaters, now often on computer and cell phone screens. YouTube, after all, is the second biggest search engine on the planet. We know what reasonable quality video looks like. Here's the good news: reasonable quality video is achievable for any church, if they plan for quality.

What Does It Take To Livestream Well?

A livestreamed worship service depends on six distinct systems. These are (1) your audio system, (2) your video system (including cameras and lights), (3) your data network, (4) some sort of control room, (5) a team of tech volunteers, and (6) a concrete ministry strategy. Without all six of these systems in place, your community will be unable to livestream worship in the stereotypical way. That is, your church will be unable to have three to four cameras in the middle of your worship space, literally streaming a live broadcast of your in-person worship service. Let us examine these systems in detail.

Audio System

Your audio system is perhaps the most important part of a livestream because audio is the most important part of video. Viewers will tolerate poor quality video with high quality audio much more readily than the reverse. If this is counterintuitive, consider which videos you will not watch on YouTube. Will you close a video first for poor quality video or poor quality audio? Fortunately, your church may have most of the components needed for a livestream already in your sanctuary.

A livestreamed worship service requires a digital audio mixer[1]. An analog audio mixer is a nonstarter for churches getting started with livestreaming. This is for a list of reasons. First, a digital mixer is much more predictable. Second, a digital mixer provides a list of extra tools that analog mixers do not have. As a practical matter, your audio will simply never be reliably good with an analog mixer. Third, a digital mixer can be controlled from another room, which is a crucial feature. We'll see more of how this works when we examine the control room. Digital mixers start around $2,400. There are slightly more affordable options, but they come with trade-offs. Perhaps your community finds an excellent deal somewhere, but this is a reasonable baseline.

Next, a livestream needs more microphones than an in-person worship service. In person, perhaps you have loud instruments that do not need a microphone, such as a piano, organ, or drum kit. However, they must have microphones for the livestream. Additionally, a livestream will want two microphones pointed at the congregation, blended in subtly to the mix. This is a crucial step in making the audio sound natural. For the purposes of this example, we will assume your church has a few extra microphones.

1. An analog mixer is probably what you think of when you imagine an audio mixer. It has lots of knobs and faders. A digital mixer may look similar, but it is actually a digital computer. If it has knobs and faders, these simply control the computer that is your digital mixer. For example, an Allen & Heath QU16 is a digital mixer, while a Mackie 1642 is an analog mixer.

Basic Costs

Allen & Heath QU16 Digital Mixer: $2,400

Microphones for everything in your worship service: We'll assume you already have these.

TOTAL: Many churches won't need upgrades here at all. The mostly likely costs are to shift to a digital mixer, and perhaps a few more microphones.

Video System

For your video system, you need to make decisions about cameras. Essentially there are two big options: PTZ cameras or cameras with a camera operator. PTZ cameras are cameras mounted on motors that can be controlled remotely. These can often be installed discreetly in a worship space, so they are relatively inobtrusive. However, they have a few big drawbacks. The most substantial drawback to PTZ cameras is their relative expense. Remember, when buying a PTZ camera, you are paying for expensive motors before you pay for nice lenses. For example, a nice looking video camera can be purchased for around $1,500. A similar image quality in a PTZ camera is closer to $5,000.

On the other hand, cameras with a camera operator can be *much* higher quality, though they require a volunteer for each camera. Because of this, I have provided three cost estimates: PTZ cameras that have a low-quality image (their image quality looks like a budget camcorder), a higher-quality PTZ camera, and one suggestion for a video camera if you have volunteers to operate them.

You might notice the cost estimates assume your community will need three cameras. Why three? This is a standard for a few reasons. If you consider switching camera angles, it is helpful to have one camera permanently on a wide angle. This provides a reliable backup, a camera option that always works, even if it isn't ideal. The second camera angle is ideal for whatever is currently happening in worship (perhaps someone is praying, or you are highlighting a musician), while the third angle shifts to prepare for whatever is next. That is, there is something immensely practical about three cameras. A church could get by with two cameras, but they are likely to see much more adjustment of cameras on-screen. This begins to chip away at the principle of communicating reasonably well in your given medium. Conversely, adding many more cameras increases complexity. In churches with more experienced volunteers this may be reasonable, but it is hardly necessary when we are beginning.

The switcher is the heart of a livestreaming system. It receives inputs from all the cameras and your PowerPoint/slides computer. It receives audio from your audio mixer. It combines all of these into your finished livestream. Then, you need a way to connect this video signal to the internet, whether you are livestreaming to YouTube or elsewhere. I often encourage faith communities to purchase The Blackmagic ATEM 1 M/E Constellation HD switcher. It is affordable, and a volunteer can be trained to operate it in seconds. This pairs nicely with the Web Presenter HD, which sends the video signal to the internet. There are alternative ways to approach this system, including doing all of this in software. In my experience, this increases complexity while reducing reliability, without saving much money.

Finally, we must consider how we create lyrics for our in-person worship, along with superimposed lyrics in our livestream. If your community still uses PowerPoint for in-person worship, this will need to be replaced. I appreciate FaithLife Proclaim, because I find it easier to train volunteers on this than alternatives like ProPresenter. These more advanced software options, and a few of their competitors, can create an independent output designed to be layered on top of your cameras.

One final subject that needs to be considered, though we are overlooking it here, is your lighting. Cameras need much more light than you might expect. What seems quite reasonable in person can be quite dim for a camera, severely degrading video quality. However, the costs for lighting can vary dramatically based on a particular worship space, making it difficult to provide reasonable estimates here.

Video System

Blackmagic ATEM 1 M/E Constellation HD Switcher: $995

BlackMagic Web Presenter HD Streaming Interface: $495

Yearly Subscription to FaithLife Proclaim (PowerPoint Alternative): $225

Various cables: $500

Camera Option 1 (PTZ Low-end):

(3) BirdDog P100 PTZ cameras: $4,485 total

Camera Option 2 (PTZ upgrade):

(3) Canon N500 PTZ cameras: $16,197 total

Camera Option 3 (with a camera operator):

(3) BlackMagic Studio Camera: $7,035 total

TOTAL: $6,000–$18,000

Data Network

Almost all churches have internet access, at least in their church office. Minimally, this needs to be extended into the tech booth in your worship space, and whatever space you use for a control room.

By the time you are doing this, most churches find it advantageous to simply provide public Wi-Fi throughout the facility. This provides a valuable resource for children's ministry, Bible studies, and other gatherings that use the campus, in addition to providing a service increasingly expected in all public spaces.

I have seen estimates to have an independent company install a network that range from $15,000 to $25,000. However, much of this expense is simply running cables. If your church can organize a group of volunteers to run cables and conduit, this expense can be cut in half, or better. Below, I suggest some typical hardware from a company that makes enterprise-level networking solutions available at very affordable prices.

The speed of your internet connection is of paramount importance, of course. A livestream needs an *upload* speed of at least 10Mbps.[2] Notice, this is the upload speed, not the more widely advertised download speed. For many types of internet connections, the upload speed and download speed are different, and the download speed is typically much higher. Ensure your connection can be at least 10Mbps, or your church will be simply be unable to livestream well. If your connection is close to 10Mbps, there are technical solutions that can provide some breathing room.

I am sometimes asked if a cell phone hotspot can provide enough bandwidth to livestream. Strictly speaking, a good 4G connection can do the job, but this misunderstands the role of the network. This computer network will allow your livestream to access the internet, of course. It also allows an iPad to talk to your audio mixer. It also allows a computer to talk to your switcher. It also allows you to have a control room somewhere else in the building, where audio can be mixed reliably for the livestream. That is, it's not just the internet connection; your community needs a robust internal LAN as well. There are solutions to make this work, but they should be avoided, if at all possible.

Basic Costs

These ranges vary primarily based on the size and physical layout of your building

Unifi Routing & Switching Equipment: $1,000–$3,000

Unifi Access Points: $500–$1,000

Cable & Conduit: $1,000–$5,000

Totals: $2,500–$9,000

2. There is a difference between 10 Mbps and 10 MBps. The latter is 8 times as fast as the former, as it is 10 megabytes per second, instead of ten megabits per second.

Control Room

A control room exists because of one simple fact: it is almost impossible to mix the audio for your livestream while you are sitting in your worship space. Even with great headphones, a person can never truly hear *just* the livestream and recognize the difference between what is in their headphones and what they are simply hearing acoustically in the room. It is extremely helpful if someone mixes the audio for your livestream in a different room. At the same time, the person mixing audio for your live worship service must be in the worship space!

While larger production facilities, and many churches, create a dedicated room for this, which also incorporates the video switching role, this is not strictly necessary. It could be placed in your church office, for example. What is necessary is to have a space somewhere in your facility where a person can watch your livestream, with a reasonable monitoring system, while controlling your digital audio mixer via iPad. That is, while one volunteer is mixing the audio for your live worship service by physically touching your audio mixer, another volunteer is controlling a distinct part of the audio mixer via iPad in an entirely different room.

Basic Costs

iPad: $329

Video Conversion: $1,500

Audio Monitoring System: $800

40" TV: $200

Cabling: $500

Total: $3,329

Tech Volunteers

By now, it should be clear that a quality livestream takes a team of volunteers. The smallest practical team is about four volunteers each Sunday. You need: one person on the audio mixer, one person on the camera switcher, one person on your PowerPoint/ProPresenter/slide computer, and one more in your control room, mixing audio for the livestream. Ideally, you also have a tech director coordinating these volunteers, but you can get away with only the four. Notice that this does not include camera operators. If you include camera operators, this number rises again (this is why so many churches choose PTZ cameras in spite of their lower image quality). Of course, four volunteers on any given Sunday means you need a roster of eight to twelve volunteers on a tech team.

Ministry Strategy

All of these technical concerns are important, but none of it matters without a ministry strategy. That is, how will you use your livestream to create community and foster worship for the audience you are trying to reach? After all, the simple existence of a livestream does not create community. A church needs a plan for this, with online hosts or digital pastors, a related social media strategy, and the like.

One mistake many churches make is to divide their audience. They provide a stream on Facebook *and* YouTube, for example. This reduces the number of viewers in either chat community. Some chat on YouTube, but they do not interact with those viewing on Facebook. If that same church would merge their entire online community into one place, this would enhance the number of participants, and increase the sense of community. To say it another way, it is easier to get conversation going with more people in the same place.

Another common issue is churches who do not control their own platform. Consider problems churches have streaming through Facebook, which regularly mutes livestreams. Facebook's automatic copyright infringement algorithms are famously faulty, and many churches each Sunday find themselves muted with no recourse (have you ever tried reaching out to Meta's tech support?). This also happens on YouTube and a few other streaming platforms, though less often. If the church did not stream through these platforms, these things would not be issues.

Instead, churches are much wiser to host their livestream on their own website. Then, put links to that worship service on social media platforms. Depending on how you organize this on the back end, this might automatically put your worship services on YouTube.[3] In other variations, you will need to upload that each Sunday. After all, you *do* want your worship services on YouTube, you just do not want YouTube to control your platform.

This can be done with a free service called the Church Online Platform. The Church Online Platform essentially creates an interface that appears to be part of your website. In the backend, you can connect most online video sources to be the actual video that is shown. The Church Online Platform has chat features, so your community can communicate with each other during worship. It has features to support prayer requests, online donations, and other useful interactions. Moving a livestream (or many other forms of online worship) to The Church Online Platform is a substantial step forward, strategically.

Finally, to have your entire livestream community in one place allows your community to leverage the insights and wisdom found throughout this book. To gather your community in one place allows you to leverage volunteers who engage with prayer, or genuinely connect with people.

Summary

From this, we can see that livestreaming reasonably well costs somewhere between $15,000 and $30,000, requires a team of eight

3. This can be done with a service like Resi or Boxcast. Both of these services host your video stream. Then, you embed your video stream in your website using a service like the Church Online Platform.

to twelve tech volunteers and a team of digital ministry hosts. Again, this is basic but quality equipment. This is robust equipment that leans heavily into the "it's amazing this is now available at this price!" approach. Fortunately, the quality of semiprofessional equipment has improved dramatically in the last decade in almost every category.

One objection to this might be that your congregation is not a megachurch and does not wish to operate like a megachurch. You should not worry about this. If you are beginning at the level described above, you will not be in any danger of appearing to be a megachurch! You will simply represent your in-person community reasonably well in a livestream. It would take years of your volunteers improving, and quite a few changes in most communities, to resemble a megachurch.

A second response to this objection might be to clarify what it is about the approach of a megachurch you find so distasteful. Many of our communities have philosophical reasons to doubt we can be in effective community with five thousand other people. Others are at odds with the typically evangelical theology of megachurches. I understand both perspectives and generally agree with them. In practice though, we often simply equate quality communication, good graphic design, and modern technology with megachurches. This conflation undermines our churches and their ability to participate in modern society.

Others might object to the video equipment I suggest as a baseline. After all, some companies make $100 cameras that can be controlled via cell phone! Surely this would lower the expense of a livestream from the $15–30,000 I suggest to somewhere well under $1,000. It is true, companies like Meevo do make cameras like this. However, I would suggest anyone considering this approach go watch the livestream of a church that takes this approach. It will quickly be obvious that this approach is poorly suited to livestreaming a worship service. The low quality of these cameras, the low quality of the audio, and the inability to place them in ideal locations undermines our assumptions about communicating reasonably well in our chosen medium.

Alternative Approaches

For some of our communities, it is now clear that livestreaming our Sunday worship service is unrealistic. That is clarifying! For others, we realize that livestreaming is not the approach we wish to take for strategic reasons. What alternatives exist?

While this book is filled with alternatives to livestreaming a worship service, I would like to highlight a few approaches that require far fewer resources. These approaches take a few hours from church staff and volunteers but can otherwise be done with cell phones and less than a thousand dollars of microphones, tripods, and lights.

The first option is Zoom meetings. Zoom meetings are a powerful tool for groups of perhaps four to twelve people. Many successful small groups, Bible studies, or book studies meet via Zoom. If run well, these meetings foster relationship and create robust community. If we compare this to our three audiences, though, we will see that Zoom meetings meet certain audiences more effectively than others. Zoom meetings are not particularly inviting to those who have no connection to your worshipping community. They are somewhat difficult to advertise to the general public, and they demand a lot of a person attending for the first time. They might meet the needs of those who wish to attend Sunday morning, but have limited availability. Perhaps most encouraging, Zoom can be a way to form excellent community, if you expect the community to stand on its own. Many of the examples in this book resonate with this approach.

Consider an alternative approach. Imagine that once a week, the pastor and lead musician sit together in the pastor's office for fifteen minutes. The musician plays a song, and the pastor summarizes "three key takeaways" of their Sunday morning sermon, before the musician plays one more song. That is the entire video. You might prerecord it one day when your musician and the pastor are both at church. Naturally, this would need to be later in the week, so the pastor has some sense of their sermon! Then you would post the video on Sunday night or Monday morning. This could be done with minimal editing, and provide a video families could use when their schedule permits. Alternatively, you could do this live on Monday morning, and have the musician read prayer requests submitted via chat. The pastor and the musician then pray together for the prayer requests after the sermon, giving the digital congregation time to submit prayer requests.

If your audience is people who are considering a visit to your in-person community, these models meet their interests quite well. They will meet the pastor and get some sense of the church community. If the audience is parishioners who want to attend Sunday morning but are unable to, this weekly video would be most life-giving! Families could watch it at a time that fits their schedule, while homebound individuals could do the same. It is a bit more difficult to see this model forming the basis of a distinct online community, though perhaps that is a lack of imagination on my part.

Best of all, each of these approaches can be taken for under a thousand dollars. Your community already has a few cell phones capable of livestreaming video, or computers and iPads if you prefer Zoom. A cell phone will require a tripod, and perhaps microphones like the Deity Pocket Wireless or VMic D3, both of which are well under $200. One might find a room with large windows, or perhaps spend a few hundred dollars on lighting.

Conclusion

Before investing in a digital ministry, we must begin with a plan. There are varied ways to approach a digital ministry, and each approach has certain benefits and drawbacks. If we begin with an assumption that a livestreamed worship service is what digital ministry means, we commit ourselves to big investments while overlooking effective alternatives. For some worshipping communities, this is the right strategy. Livestreamed worship works for many churches! I hope, though, this has helped consider alternatives which might meet our strategic goals more effectively. Some of these alternative approaches have improved potential to form relationships and build community.

Stephen Hale (he/him) After decades of working in churches, Stephen started a production company. Capital Hope Media helps nonprofits and churches communicate with their followers and tell their stories well. Stephen regularly consults with churches on their digital ministry, combining a background in pastoral ministry with decades of experience in audiovisual technology. He is husband to Mary, father to Stephanie, and devotee of Tony's Coffee.

IO

Steps to Practically Create
a Digital Ministry

John Grosso

When Pope Francis slowly crossed an empty Saint Peter's Square—alone and in the pouring rain—on that fateful day in March 2020, the enormity of what was occurring throughout the world struck me in a way that rendered me silent and frightened.

It is not that I was unaware of the horror of the situation in which we had all found ourselves. Like many, I had anxiously followed the news since the *novel coronavirus* was first discovered, locked down with my wife as COVID-19 reached our shores, and religiously followed the developments on television and digital media. By March 27, 2020, the Roman Catholic diocese for which I worked had already suspended the public celebration of Mass, dispensed the faithful from their Sunday obligation, and my colleagues and I had worked long hours to move all our worship online.

And yet, I was struck so deeply, so profoundly, so strongly in the depths of my soul by every step the Holy Father took, every word he preached, and every drop of rain that fell on the cobblestones and the crucifix alike. Though I thought it had been clear before, with each passing moment I could not shake a singular feeling: *This is different. There is no going back from this.*

Given that my tradition, as a devout Catholic, is an inherently sacramental faith, I struggled internally with how to translate the transcendental nature of our worship—that needs to be experienced in person—to an online medium. How can you accompany someone whose hand you cannot grasp? How can you sit before the Lord in adoration when a digital screen, and likely many miles, keep you apart? How can we spiritually feed people when they are unable to receive the Eucharist (which Catholics believe is the true body and blood of Christ)? The list goes on and on.

As though he was reading my mind (and likely millions of others), Pope Francis concluded his remarks with this:

> *Embracing his (Jesus') cross means finding the courage to embrace all the hardships of the present time, abandoning for a moment our eagerness for power and possessions in order to make room for the creativity that only the Spirit is capable of inspiring. It means finding the courage to create spaces where everyone can recognize that they are called, and to allow new forms of hospitality, fraternity, and solidarity.*

It was upon that rock—a foundation of creativity, hospitality, solidarity, and fraternity—that we built our digital media strategy during COVID-19, and where I would suggest anyone looking to build a digital media ministry first start.

When COVID-19 forced us to pause public worship and discouraged large gatherings to safeguard and protect human life, digital media professionals that worked for the Church had to get creative while remaining steadfast in our faith and traditions. Though that may sound imposing (how can you be creative when you have nearly two millennia of tradition to build upon?), there is a great deal of freedom and peace that comes with knowing and understanding "the rules of engagement" that come with tradition.

Instead, the challenge came from not being prepared. Though digital media ministry had been expanding rapidly in the Catholic tradition, there was not a widespread practice of livestreaming

Mass, creating and maintaining digital communities, or providing spiritual accompaniment online. So, when the pandemic hit our shores like a tidal wave, we were faced with the overnight reality of not being equipped for the kind of ministry that our people needed. In short, we were thrust into the breach with one hand tied behind our backs.

I pray that such a situation does not present itself during the ministry of anyone reading this resource, but if COVID-19 has taught us anything, it is that people are online and using these digital spaces now, and we must reach out to them there. It is important that we know who they are, how many might be out there, and the best avenues to reach them. Start now: ask around during physical gatherings, spend some time researching what platforms are working for other religious traditions in the area, or where certain age demographics like to digitally linger. A shepherd must know everything they can about their sheep—and digital media is no different.

Creativity, Intentionality, and Discernment

As you begin to understand the digital landscape before you, you can begin to get creative. Is there a hunger for livestreaming services among your congregation? Are people looking for spiritual encouragement throughout the day, but don't have a lot of time? Does your flock not have a digital space they feel they can safely go to in between worship services? Understanding your flock, their needs, and their wants, will allow you to be creative in responding to those needs.

Early in the COVID-19 pandemic, few of the parishes that I work with were equipped for livestreaming services. As we scrambled to install systems that could accomplish that in a professional, automated, and reverent way, our fearless and devoted priests went to work. Priests were taping or livestreaming Masses from their offices or the rectory, making videos to update and reassure their parishioners, hearing confessions while penitents were in their cars outside in the parking lot, and streaming hours and hours of adoration, sacred music, and more. Parish ministries began to meet on Zoom. One priest even filmed himself singing a traditional Irish blessing on Saint Patrick's Day.

In each situation, the clergy took great care to do small, intentional things to make sacred the space, both digital and physical, where people would be tuning in for worship. Often, this was as simple as an altar cloth on a desk, music being streamed in during times a hymn would be sung, or a priest spending a few more precious seconds in silence as he elevated the body of Christ to his digital congregation.

In short, this creativity was not grandiose, nor was it irreverent or done for the sake of spectacle. It was intentional, simple, and relational. Priests and those who assisted them with such outreach asked their congregations what else they might like to see, and how best they could minister to them and sit with them.

Some congregations asked for fireside chats with their clergy, and their clergy responded to that and held them. Some congregations wanted daily Mass livestreamed, or others a novena prayed. You never know what your community needs until you ask them, which is the first and most essential step of discernment. In other words: "ask, and you shall receive."

From these interactions, clergy and laity were able to engage in mutual discernment for their communities, and though we were separated from one another and from our sacraments, there was a palpable and contagious sense of community, empathy, and unity.

Create Sacred Digital Space

There was a moment of realization that came after this initial phase of "figuring it out" that happened sometime around Easter 2020. When it became apparent that the pandemic was going to be here for the long haul, and that even after vaccination, digital worship was going to be a permanent fixture of all that we do, parishes had to recalibrate.

Those who were able to move the livestreams of Mass to their church buildings did so, allowing the faithful to feel as though they were back in their spiritual home. Equipment was overhauled: higher quality internet, cameras, and sound were all prioritized so that if the faithful were to participate in digital worship, it would be done with beauty, reverence, dignity, and the intentionality it deserves.

This felt like a turning point as parishes, led by their clergy and staff, made a permanent and lasting commitment to digital media ministry in a way that did not replace physical gatherings, but enhanced it. Though some parishes perhaps could not afford the "high-end camera" or lacked the ability to tap into an "ancient" sound system, they were able to enhance their digital ministry in small ways. This sent a message to their congregations that was irrefutable and resonates deeply to this day: "We will not abandon you. If this is where you are, then this is where we will be too. We are in this together with you."

Since then, there has been a temptation to label digital media as a pandemic necessity and nothing more, a Band-Aid to be discarded once used and never engaged with again. Though I can understand that these ideas come from a desire to return to "normalcy," the fact remains that there is no going back to the pre-pandemic landscape. Even if it doesn't look exactly like it did during the pandemic lockdown, digital media is here to stay, and we must learn how to effectively minister in these spaces.

Seek Moments of Digital Encounter

The key to digital media ministry is meeting people where they are and loving them. This is no different from any other Christian ministry—just that "where people are" is Facebook, Twitter, Instagram, or generally online. If we seek to encounter people, meet them, understand them, and love them, are we not doing precisely what Jesus commands us to do in the Gospels?

As someone who spent an enormous amount of time surveying the digital landscape before, during, and after the COVID-19 pandemic, there is a lot that I have learned and observed from different parishes, religious traditions, and even secular organizations that strove to create "sacred" digital space. (Professional sports teams, lifestyle brands, and even Disney come to mind).

Your digital media ministry will not bear fruit if it speaks but doesn't listen; if you build a podium and not a forum; and if you seek only to draw people to an event, gathering, website, or donation page. Not that these are not worthy causes or important for ministry! Of course, it's important—vital, even—that the faithful hear prophetic sermons, understand what events or ministries the Church has built for them, and give to support the faith community. These considerations just cannot be the entirety or end goal of your digital ministry, or you will not reach those who need you.

Instead, provide spaces for your community to digitally gather—perhaps in a group on a prominent social media site, or a feedback box in your email newsletter. Perhaps your website can serve as a digital bulletin board, highlighting and featuring the stories of fellow community members. Or perhaps you can host a weekly livestream where all who have prayer intentions may gather together to lift them up to heaven.

Reducing people to seats to fill at an event or money raised towards a goal (no matter how noble your intentions) robs them of their dignity as a human person—a dignity that exists while they are using or participating in digital space just as it does when they sit before you physically.

It's okay if occasionally at the end of a digital media service, you share an upcoming event, or voice a community need that requires volunteers or donations. But if a parishioner were to find your Facebook page and see nothing but flyers for events, donation requests, and low-resolution pictures of a poorly attended function, what kind of spiritual growth can they expect to achieve from that? Why would they want to digitally affiliate with such a space that doesn't value them as a person?

Accompany People on Their Journey of Faith

The journey of faith is a lifelong one we affirm and recommit to each day, and many of us can point to the people who have accompanied us along the path. Parents, mentors, friends, clergy, spiritual leaders, and many others have walked with us in times of triumph and of turmoil, physically accompanying us to services, to the sacraments, and to personal encounters with Christ Himself.

As clergy reading this book, you are no doubt well-versed in the importance of accompaniment in your day-to-day ministry. To be blunt, it is time to take what you've learned and apply it to digital media.

If people are spending time in the vast digital wilderness, alone, exposed to the vitriol, hatred, anger, and scandal that permeates the most challenging corners of the internet, it is our duty as people of faith to bring the light of Christ to these places. After all, what shepherd leaves their sheep to fend for themselves in the wilderness?

On the road to Emmaus, Jesus walked with His disciples in the wrong direction for hours, meeting them where they were in their despair and depression, and lifting them up throughout their journey by recounting the history of salvation. It was only after He made Himself known in the breaking of bread that the disciples rushed back to Jerusalem, where they were needed.

By no means is anyone advocating frequenting the frontiers of the internet proselytizing (though some of us are called to be that "voice crying out in the wilderness"). Instead, provide a digital hand to those who walk the journey of faith online by being present to them. Sometimes, making a commitment to updating your website frequently, using high-quality images or graphics, and engaging daily with the faithful is all you need. Keep it simple— regular and daily communication that your social media followers can come to expect and rely on is a good start. Praying for them daily and allowing the Lord to work through you to share with them what they may need to hear that day online is another way that you can accompany your flock. To the extent that you are able, using high-quality images, video, graphics, and proofread captions show your digital community that you value them, you value this medium, and you are willing to put in the effort to make communications to them reverent and beautiful.

Once you have identified the needs of your community through listening, discernment, and engaging conversation, you will be better prepared to walk with them on their journey of faith in more specific ways.

During the most acute phases of the COVID-19 pandemic, I knew of many priests who "tried everything." During weekly check-in sessions held on Facebook Live during the initial "lockdown" many parishioners were first cautious about interacting with their clergy in this new medium. But when clergy and staff made themselves continually available, normalizing this form of communications, and shared their fears and prayers in a vulnerable, but not inappropriate way, the suggestions and asks came pouring in.

One community asked if they could "attend Mass in their cars" once restrictions eased up, and for over a year, a pastor celebrated Mass from the roof of his church, livestreaming it for those who were parked in the back of their lot, and purchasing a radio transmitter so that people could hear the liturgy. He did this even in times of bitter cold or unrelenting sun, renting a scissor lift, ensuring the music used was licensed appropriately, and consulting with parishioners on his Facebook page every step of the way.

Another priest used digital media to ask parishioners how he could help them receive the Eucharist as many continued to stay away from large gatherings. Because of the relationship that he had built with the community, they felt comfortable asking him to come out—to their houses, to street corners, to their decks, to parks, and beyond. He said Masses for the faithful outside everywhere he could, and it was all made possible because of the dynamic of trust, suspension of judgement, and spirit of inclusion with which he approached digital ministry.

During Holy Week of 2020, when our churches were unavailable for public worship and in deep mourning at the inability to participate in the sacred Triduum, the bishops and priests of dioceses around the world made special livestream accommodations—streaming every service from the Chrism Mass to Stations of the Cross, to the great Easter Vigil. For a scared and traumatized world, seeing the paschal candle lit and hearing the proclamation that Jesus is risen ring out in the empty cathedral was the peace and consolation they needed.

Growing and Maintaining Your Digital Community

Learning about your community and speaking to them in an authentic way will undoubtedly make you a more effective communicator and digital minister—and word spreads fast. People will share with others that they are being fulfilled and fed in these digital spaces, and with that comes growth—first slowly and steadily, but then fast and furious. To be prepared for this, it's important to get yourself into the habit of best practices.

If you have a "group" community on Facebook, LinkedIn, or another medium, make sure you are checking on them daily. Make sure you are responding to questions or concerns, even the negative ones, in a timely manner. Digital media ministry, much like in-person ministry, is all about building mutual trust and understanding.

Set a dedicated day for your email newsletter to go out—and make sure your website is updated with seasonal pictures, news, and events from your church. Allow it to be a spiritual home for your parishioners, much as the church is their physical home.

It's also important to allow people the safe space to be upset with you, with the Church, or with something happening in their lives. Equally important is the need to ensure these people feel heard in their moment of frustration, while also ensuring they do not dissuade others from commenting or engaging. This is often a hard line to walk, but it is essential for digital media ministry.

In one of the Facebook groups that I managed, we had a very open and transparent rules policy. People were allowed to gripe or complain, even vent their frustrations, but if in an argument they resorted to ad hominem attacks; used words that are pointed, targeted, or inappropriate; or deliberately spread misinformation, they were gently but firmly corrected and reminded of the rules. If they did it a second time, their comments were removed, and they were spoken to privately—and warned that the next infraction will result in a temporary pause in their ability to engage. This was not meant as a punishment, but as a time-out that allowed for reflection and introspection, a time to cool off. It was also a clear demonstration to the community that any posting that harms their dignity or dissuades them from active participation is not okay. It was also a clear sign to the rest of the world, who may stumble upon these conversations between people of faith, that this is not how a Christian should behave.

Correcting misinformation and knowing when someone needs to be temporarily separated (and spoken with privately) from the online community is often a judgement or a "gut" call but can be one of the most important things you can do—not just for your community, but for the offending individual.

Of course, there should always be an opportunity for repentance and readmission to a social media group, page, or other digital space. We are to be merciful like the Father, and Jesus' command to forgive our brothers not just seven times, but "seventy times seven."

As people become more accustomed to and comfortable with engaging in these digital spaces, watch something truly remarkable happen. Digital culture, friendships, and genuine community will form before your very eyes.

People will recognize each other, and may even become personal friends on social media, exchanging direct messages sharing their lives and encouraging comments. Some of the parishes I worked with had "regulars" attending daily Mass online, many who had never attended in person, that began to know each other. During the sign of peace, the chat on the Mass livestream on Facebook would be flooded with "peace be with you!" and "so good to see you!" from jovial and genuinely appreciative parishioners who were just happy to take some time out of their day to pray and be with others who shared their faith.

One situation that I'll never forget: during the time in which the obligation to attend Sunday Mass was dispensed, the diocese would send out a beautifully recorded Mass celebrated by the bishop at 8:00 AM every Sunday. On the very rare occasions when distribution would be even one minute late due to a technical error, emails or phone calls would come in from very well-intentioned people saying: "Is Mass live yet? I look forward to this every Sunday!"

In some of the parishes I have worked with, parish ministries that would otherwise attract a moderate group of people in person during weeknight gatherings would be bursting at the seams when meeting via Zoom. One parishioner said it bluntly during a meeting of young adults: "I can't sit through thirty minutes of traffic on a Tuesday night after being away from my kids all day, but I sure can flip a switch, log on to Zoom, and join you in my sweatpants!" Communities like these parish ministries take on a different life and likely experience some growing pains as we make hybrid accommodations, but if even one more person is reached because of this accessibility, isn't it worth it?

Two Notes of Caution

Though I am a staunch and fervent advocate for digital media ministry, it would be naïve to say that in embarking on this journey you will face no problems or adversity. In that spirit, I would offer you two notes of caution as you discern a pathway forward that works for your community.

In my experience, much like the rest of the world these past years, Christian denominations have all buckled under the strain of the rampant polarization, fake news, vitriol, and an all-out digital assault on the dignity of the human person. It feels nearly impossible these days to comment on anything, let alone participate in civil discourse, without the situation devolving into tribalism and division.

Assuming the best intentions of people, setting firm boundaries and rules of engagement, and reminding people that behind the screen name, avatar, or icon is a real living and breathing human with struggles and challenges are all the antidotes to these poisons. However, those antidotes must be provided continuously, intentionally, and mercifully.

Conflict is unavoidable online, just as it is in real life. Entrusting our communities to good shepherds, ensuring we are equipped with conflict resolution skills and de-escalation tactics, and praying that God will help us in our struggles can heal whatever ails your digital community.

The other caution is a bit of repetition, but it is that important: do not treat people on digital media as merely means to an end. Though you may feel the most important thing is to get them to an event, raise money for a worthy cause, or direct them to something you have discerned they need, you cannot simply force the issue with your message. For this again we can use Jesus as our model. In passage after passage of the Gospel, we see Jesus sowing seeds of wisdom and grace, confronting people with an ask when the time was right. Though we can never know the inner workings of people's hearts the way Jesus did, we must pray for the patience to sow seeds and the wisdom to know when it is time to harvest them.

In the meantime, a successful digital media ministry focuses on the community you have before you right here, right now, and bringing those people into an encounter with Jesus Christ.

It's easy to dismiss digital life as not being real, but for many it is. These experiences, friendships, and relationships are all real to the people participating in them. If you treat people on digital media with dignity, accept them as they are, and minister to them as they need it, they are far more likely to join you in person for physical worship. In my experience, digital ministry can only truly bear fruit if there is an authentic digital community—worship is meant to be in community!

Of course, for those of us in traditions like mine, it is vital that we do not underestimate the value of physical encounter. For us in the Catholic tradition, the sacramental nature of our Church is a core tenant of who we are and how we receive grace. I remain encouraged though that we can use digital media to accompany people towards an encounter with Jesus and the Church. Digital media can be part of that journey for any believer who participates in online activity.

Even before my years in ministry, I was captivated by the beautiful, emotional, and radical act of Jesus washing the feet of His disciples during the Last Supper. I always feel the ground quake around me when I hear: *"Do you realize what I have done for you? You call me 'teacher' and 'master,' and rightly so, for indeed I am. If I, therefore, the master and teacher, have washed your feet, you ought to wash one another's feet. I have given you a model to follow, so that as I have done for you, you should also do."*

This commandment applies to every aspect of our lives as disciples of Christ, whether we are clergy or laity. Allow this to be the model we follow in digital media ministry: serving in His name, washing the feet of those whom we serve, and providing a witness of love and mercy to our communities and to the whole world.

John Grosso (he/him) serves as the Associate Director of Communications for Foundations and Donors Interested in Catholic Activities. Previously, he served as the director of digital media for the Roman Catholic Diocese of Bridgeport in Connecticut.He is also a freelance digital media consultant for religious institutions, nonprofits, and small businesses. He is a Roman Catholic speaker and author. In 2021, John was involved in the Vatican Dicastery for Communication's Faith Communication in the Digital World project. John completed his bachelor's degree at Boston College, and his master's degree at Sacred Heart University. He resides in Connecticut with his wife Nicole, daughter Rose, and Golden Retriever, Ellie.

Conclusion
The Harvest Is Great
Rev. Brandan Robertson

The future of our world is digital. Or rather, one of the futures of our world is digital. If the message of the Gospel and the healing power of Christian community is going to continue to have an impact and relevance in the centuries to come, we must meaningfully grapple with how we can translate them into a digital space. On one hand, this is not a difficult task—since the dawn of the internet, pioneers and innovators within religion have been experimenting with how to create spiritual community online, so the road map and resources are there. On the other hand, as technology continues to evolve and develop in new and innovative ways, and as humans adapt to and react to the emerging digital world, faith communities will need to be nimble and flexible—which has never been our strong suit. Yet this is a moment that we cannot afford to miss out on, one in which we can truly reach the world with the healing, inclusive, and transformative power of our faith. If we don't rise to meet this moment, others will. Time and time again, more conservative and exclusive faith communities have beat progressive communities to the technological punch and have reached millions more people with a version of faith that has perpetuated marginalization and declared that God's love and grace is limited to a select few. But following the global pandemic of COVID-19, the playing field is truly leveled. We all have learned how to engage digitally and how to create even simple virtual community spaces. Whoever you are reading this book—at this very moment, in your pocket or on a device nearby, you have the potential to reach *millions* of people *around the world* instantly with a gospel of inclusion. You can create safe and transformative spaces for people around the world who yearn for a faith community but do not have access to one geographically near them. You can produce and publish thoughtful content that can challenge and provoke people in every corner of the globe to think differently about their faith. In this dawning digital era, all of us have an opportunity to use our gifts, talents, and stories to make a real impact for the common good. The question is, will we rise to meet this moment or let it pass as others seize the opportunity that the Spirit is presenting to us?

In the book of Acts, the apostle Stephen declares that "the Most High does not live in houses made by human hands" (Acts 7:48). Throughout history, humans have clung to the illusion that our temples and sanctuaries were the holy places in which the Divine took up residence. But today, in our digital era, we can see the profound truthfulness of Stephen's words—God's presence is not limited to physical, brick-and-mortar spaces, but transcends the physical, moving in, though, and beyond time and space. God is present in the digital sanctuary, which is say, the entirety of creation. God is not limited to consecrated spaces or to ordained people, for every space and every person is sacred. All the world is a sanctuary for the Divine, and those of us who are called and invested in religious ministry must heed the call of the Spirit to curate digital sanctuaries where the divine light and love of God can be shared to all who desire to experience it. This is the most exciting time to be alive. This is the most exciting time to do ministry. The opportunities for impact are truly infinite. So don't let this moment pass. May the wisdom and experience of the practitioners in this short guide be a launching pad for your own increased digital engagement. As you step into the digital realm, may you lay aside any fear or trepidation, knowing that failure is impossible, because whether you reach twelve or 120,000 people with your digital ministry, whether it's highly produced or very "low quality", your engagement in the digital realm *will* make an impact on *somebody, somewhere* who needs it.

The harvest is truly great—may you step out into the ever-evolving digital landscape with faith, hope, love, and may many find healing through your digital sanctuary.